42: Callaghan the Monetarist.

# THE
# ALTERNATIVE
# ECONOMIC
# STRATEGY

CSE
BOOKS

Labour
Co-ordinating
Committee

# THE ALTERNATIVE ECONOMIC STRATEGY

A RESPONSE BY THE LABOUR MOVEMENT TO THE ECONOMIC CRISIS

The London CSE Group

The Alternative Economic Strategy
was first published jointly by
CSE Books, 55 Mount Pleasant, London WC1
and the Labour Co-ordinating Committee,
9 Poland St.,London W1
in October 1980.

*British Library Cataloguing in Publication Data*

Conference of Socialist Economists
London Working Group

The Alternative Economic Strategy
1. Great Britain — Economic Policy
330.9'41'085   HC256.6

ISBN 0 906336 22 8 Hb
ISBN 0 906336 23 6 Pb

Printed by Blackrose Press (TU) Ltd.
30 Clerkenwell Close, London EC1R 0AT.

Cover designed by Cliff Harper and printed by
Calvert's North Star Press (TU) Ltd.
55 Mount Pleasant, London WC1X 0AE.

# CONTENTS

# PREFACE

The next few years will be a critical period for the Left in Britain. Whatever view you take of the record of the last Labour Government, its defeat and the election of the present Conservative Government represent a major setback. The Tory Government has precipitated an economic crisis which threatens to destroy a substantial part of industry leaving between two and three million unemployed for as long as it remains in power. It has launched an attack on the gains made by the Labour movement in the post-war period in improved public services, higher living standards and strengthened trade union organisation.

In these circumstances we face a basic challenge. Can we develop and build a consensus around a socialist strategy which offers a way out of the crisis — and an alternative to the economics of Howe and of Healey? The central argument of this book is that the set of policies which have become known as the 'Alternative Economic Strategy' (AES) developed within the Labour movement as a response to the crisis, provides a framework within which we can provide jobs, higher living standards and improved public services, and initiate a transition towards socialism.

The AES is not a blueprint, nor a formula for the manipulation of technical instruments of government policy. Nor is it a set of policies which has been finalised and elaborated in detail. Rather it represents a field of debate, a consensus on the basic components and structure of economic strategy within which there is an urgent need to develop and debate more detailed policies. In this book we offer a contribution to that debate.

We believe that this debate is of central importance. The AES is not just a technical matter for economists, but raises issues which should be taken up and discussed throughout the Labour movement. We have tried to avoid technical language and obscure jargon in writing the book so we hope it will be accessible to, and of interest to, a wide range of people.

The book has been written collectively by members of the 'London Group' of the Conference of Socialist Economists (CSE), and published jointly by CSE Books and the Labour Co-ordinating Committee (LCC). The CSE was set up in 1970 to provide a forum for socialists to debate and develop analysis of the development of capitalism and problems of economic policy. The CSE publishes a journal 'Capital and Class' three times a year, while CSE Books publishes the work of CSE groups and individual members as well as providing a book club service. The Labour Co-ordinating Committee was set up in 1978 to link up Left activists in the Labour Party. It has organised a series of conferences and produced a range of publications, including its broadsheet 'Labour Activist'. A shorter pamphlet on economic strategy has recently been published. Further details can be obtained from LCC, 9, Poland St., London W1. The views expressed in this book are not necessarily the views of either the CSE or the LCC.

The London Group began studying the Alternative Economic Strategy in 1978 and has contributed papers to the Annual Conference of the CSE each year since then. One of these papers was published as 'Crisis, the Labour Movement and the Alternative Economic Strategy' in *Capital and Class* Number 8. The group is composed of economists who are active in the Labour movement. Most of the present members of the group are members of the Labour Party, but we see the ideas presented here as a possible basis for unity on the Left rather than as simply part of a debate internal to the Labour Party.

The book is the outcome of a long series of discussions in the London Group, and of wider debates in the CSE and in the LCC. The final draft has been written by five members of the Group who are deeply indebted to all those who have contributed to these discussions and in particular to those who have commented on earlier drafts of the book. Naturally no one but the authors is implicated in its conclusions. Finally, while each of the contributors supports the broad arguments put forward, we are not individually committed to all detailed points of analysis. The Group will be continuing to discuss and develop the issues raised in this book, and would welcome comments on the book and new members to the Group. We can be contacted through London CSE Group, 55 Mount Pleasant, London WC1.

# The Case for the Alternative Economic Strategy

## 1. Introduction

The key challenge facing the Labour movement and the Left is to develop an economic strategy which can provide an alternative to the present policies of Monetarism. Britain under the Tory Government is rapidly entering the most severe slump since the Great Depression. The slump is matched by serious recession in other capitalist countries, but in Britain it is likely to prove deeper and longer-lasting than anywhere else in the developed world.

This slump is not a natural calamity nor an inevitable consequence of forces beyond our control. It is not cause by the 'greed' of the oil-producing countries nor by New Technology. It is a crisis which has been aggravated by the actions of the present government. But this is not to say that it is the consequence of economic mis-management, of technical incompetence or of the stupidity of government ministers. Rather the government is pursuing a strategy designed to force a radical restructuring of industry, and of the relations between management and Labour, along capitalist lines, by greatly strengthening the operation of market forces. In other words it is seeking to undermine the organisation and bargaining strength of the trade union movement using the weapon of higher unemployment. It is in this sense that we face an economic and political crisis.

## 2. The Economic Crisis

The features of the economic crisis are clear to see. Unemployment is likely to rise above two million this winter and remain between two and three million. The output of manufacturing industry has already fallen by a tenth and is expected to continue to fall, eliminating home production in certain key sectors. Investment has collapsed, not only in manufacturing but also in housing and construction. Public services are being cut back, hitting education, health and social services. Spending on housing is planned to fall by *half* over the next four years. Living standards, after rising sharply in 1978 and '79 are beginning to fall and will continue to do so as earnings are held down below the rise in the cost of living and social benefits are cut.

These symptoms flow directly from the government's economic policies to squeeze the economy by cutting public spending while increasing the tax burden, by controlling credit and boosting interest rates, and by maintaining the pound at an overvalued level so that exports are cut and imports are increased.

But it would be wrong to see these policies as based simply on arbitrary vindictiveness or on mistaken economic theory. They reflect a view that a radical departure is necessary in order to lay the basis for future expansion. Britain remains a fundamentally capitalist economy. This means that it shares with other capitalist economies two basic characteristics. First, production is organised through markets on which goods are exchanged. Second, the means of production—the factories, offices and machines—are owned by one group or class who employs a second group. It is from these simple characteristics that we can derive certain conclusions which provide a framework for understanding the economic crisis we face today.

The first conclusion is that the product of the economy is divided between the incomes of those who are employed (wages) and a surplus (profit). This division is necessarily made through conflict, which takes the form of a bargain over the level of wages and continual struggle over the intensity of work between management (which naturally seeks to get the maximum output for the wages it has paid) and the workforce. We refer generally to the interests of profit as 'Capital' and the interests of wages as 'Labour'. A basic characteristic of capitalism is 'class struggle' between Capital and Labour.

A second conclusion is that the progress of capitalism is likely to be highly uneven. The market operates by driving inefficient producers out of business which can be disruptive. But the main cause is the nature of the labour market, which regulates the balance of forces in the conflict between Capital and Labour. High unemployment for example, weakens the position of Labour. A capitalist system is marked by periods of expansion followed by periods of contraction or 'crisis', in which unemployment rises, forcing down wages and increasing profit, and in which inefficient firms are forced out of business, allowing profitable growth or 'accumulation' to take place once more.

All this may appear to some readers as obvious and to others as crude and contentious. The latter critics we hope to convince in Chapter 3 where we develop these general propositions about capitalism to take into account the numerous specific characteristics of British capitalism in the post-war period. Running through this book is a view that this framework of understanding is valuable in accounting for present developments. Briefly the government has been forced to precipitate an economic crisis in a slightly desperate, but nonetheless rational attempt to lay the basis for future growth under capitalist conditions. The precondition for the success of this strategy is the defeat or decisive weakening of the Labour movement.

## 3. The Political Crisis

The economic crisis has an important political dimension. The policies of the present government mark a clear break with the political consensus within which politics has been conducted in the post-war period in Britain. We refer to this consensus as the Keynes-Beveridge consensus to indicate its dual foundation in a commitment to manage the economy in pursuit of certain agreed economic objectives, including a high level of employment, and in a steady expansion of the social and welfare services which go to make up the welfare state.

These foundations proved unable to bear the weight of the edifice constructed upon them. Ultimately the consensus was contingent on continued growth to meet rising aspirations and a tacit acceptance by Labour that it would not use its increased bargaining strength to appropriate an increasing share of total income. Through the sixties and seventies the Labour movement was able to take advantage of high levels of employment to consolidate its strength—unmatched in any other industrial country—both nationally and at the shop-floor level. But the strength developed was essentially defensive, and the more aggressive it became—paradoxically—the more its defences were weakened. Militant wage struggles or firm control over the process of production for example proved self-defeating as long as the levers of control over investment, production, pricing and employment decisions remained firmly in capitalist hands.

By the end of the seventies there was a stalemate in the balance of class forces. Capital, already weakened by the world crisis, was unable to undertake the drastic restructuring of industry necessary for it to restore its place in the world economy, and Labour was unwilling to make concessions beyond restraint in wages. Tory monetarism is an attempt to break this stalemate at the expense of Labour.

The disintegration of the basis of the Keynes-Beveridge consensus removed the basis of the economics of Social Democracy: its limitations became clearly exposed. Once expanded social programmes are crossed off the social-democratic agenda, the residue has little attraction. Incomes policy, effectively wage restraint, remains, followed by special employment measures, subsidies to industry and the now obligatory gesture in the direction of the Third World. The whole is drawn together by a touching faith in the operation of 'the market' as the guardian of social welfare. The truth is that such a programme is bankrupt in the face of the profound crisis we are now entering; that the 'market' is largely dominated by the actions of a couple of hundred companies, mostly multinational in operations, and all international in perspective; and that social regulation through the market offers only hardship and wasted resources. The choices are perhaps more clear than they have been in the past.

If we are to develop a credible, viable and popular alternative to Tory monetarism it must offer a far more radical programme than that offered by Social Democracy. It must be an alternative which is founded on a far sounder understanding of the nature of the crisis; which seeks not to work within the constraints imposed by the logic of the capitalist economy but to transform those constraints; which is not dependent on shackling the Labour movement but which releases its strength to achieve far greater social control over production. In short, we need an alternative socialist economic strategy.

## 4. A Socialist Alternative

The disintegration of political consensus is mirrored in a crisis of equal proportions in socialist thinking. After a decade of intense activity in which conditions could hardly have been better for the development of a broad socialist movement, the Left remains fragmented and, in many ways, politically isolated. Two positive developments offer hope for the future. The first is a growing willingness to think beyond the 'How and Why' of Socialism, to go beyond the abstract polarisation of revolution and reform, or of insurrectionary and parliamentary positions, and to study the *forms of transition*, and the ways in which the outcome is conditioned by the means of its achievement.

The second positive development is a growing dissatisfaction with 'textbook socialism', a dissatisfaction with schematic analysis and simple application of models of political organisation and political practice, bequeathed from movements operating in circumstances quite different from those we face today. In discussing an alternative socialist economic strategy these are issues we need to consider. We must also ask in what sense the AES is a transitional strategy for developing the economy in a socialist direction.

We return to these questions in more detail in the concluding Chapter but it is worth anticipating at this stage two counter arguments. The first is that discussion of an alternative economic strategy is premature when the real political task is to defend jobs, living standards, public services and trade union rights against the attacks made by the Tories. But we would argue that the most trenchant weapon in the Tories' propaganda armoury is the suggestion that there *is no alternative*. Unless the Labour movement sets out clearly and in some detail a comprehensive and viable socialist economic strategy which is not simply based on slogans and worn formulae then there is much truth in this allegation. This is in no way to underplay the importance of defensive struggles, merely to say that the greatest enemy of defensive strength is the apathy born out of fatalism.

Another possible criticism is that our emphasis on the need for *economic* strategy neglects the role of politics. Economics it may be suggested is a secondary matter best left to the economists while the real business of developing political consciousness gets under way. We make no claims that an economic programme should exhaust the content of a socialist strategy. But we do argue that without a programme which responds to people's basic concerns with job security, the cost of living, housing availability and the level of pensions and child benefits, socialist appeals will be regarded with justifiable suspicion. These are the issues of economic strategy; they are of vital concern to us all. Significant advances will never be made if economic strategy is left to 'the experts'.

In short there are three kinds of questions to which we relate discussion of economic strategy. How can we best defend ourselves in the crisis? How can we develop an economic alternative to bring a resolution of the crisis in the interests of the working class? Is such an alternative the basis of a transition towards a socialist economy?

## 5. The Alternative Economic Strategy

We will argue that a consensus has developed in recent years in the Labour movement around a set of policies – termed loosely the 'Alternative Economic Strategy' (AES) – which provides a starting point for answering these questions. The basic elements of the AES can be set out simply:

* A policy for expansion aimed at restoring full employment and raising living standards, based on a planned reflation of the economy primarily through increases in public spending.
* Planned controls on foreign trade and international capital movements to protect the balance of payments and prevent flight of capital.
* An industrial strategy based on extended public ownership (including financial institutions), and planning at the level of the firm through Planning Agreements tied to an extensive network of industrial democracy.
* A national economic plan coordinating macroeconomic policies with industrial planning.
* Control of inflation based on price control.

Different variants of this basic strategy have received consistent support from TUC and Labour Party conferences over the last few years. In addition, individual trade unions have elaborated different parts of the strategy in their publications and campaigns. It is this consensus, in spite of the significant differences of interpretation that exist, that makes the AES such an important unifying strategy.

How has it developed? The basic elements of the industrial strategy were worked out inside the Labour Party in Opposition in 1970-74, and the demand for trade controls was added in 1975. With the 1976 sterling crisis and pressure from the IMF, the Labour Government opted decisively for a strategy of further deflation and public expenditure cuts. The AES then came to be articulated as a coherent alternative to the Government's change of direction. Some political content was injected by the lesson of the failure of the government to implement the industrial policies pressed by the Labour Party, but the politics of the strategy have generally remained underdeveloped. There has also been little serious discussion of the economics of the strategy – which is commonly, and inaccurately, identified with import controls plus a 'Bennite' industrial policy.

In the last decade the trade union movement has developed enormously as a political force. It has moved far beyond the confines of wage negotiation to intervene extensively in economic policy formation and in legislation on a wide range of subjects. By no means could all such involvements be considered progressive.

There is a constant threat of incorporation and co-option of trade union leaders who may succumb to the blandishments of personal privilege or to the peculiar processes of institutionalisation which bring responsibility without power. Nonetheless, the movement has gained enormously in the range and sophisitication of its thinking on economic and social policy. Inevitably divisions arise as conflicts of interest are reflected in policy prescription. Public sector unions have had different concerns from primarily industrial unions, skilled or craft unions from general unions. These were perhaps most obvious and most damaging in 1976 when the industrial unions appeared to accept the logic that public expenditure cuts were necessary in order to free resources that were being 'crowded out' of industrial investment. Incomes policy is another issue on which there are fundamental disagreements. There are in fact widely divergent views in the Labour movement as to the political content of economic strategy. We return to this question in Chapter 11.

Thus in confronting the basic challenge with which we began to provide an alternative to monetarism we take as our starting point the policies that have won wide support within the Labour movement in the last few years. However, it *is* just a starting point for we see it as essential both to discuss and develop the economics of the AES and to deepen and strengthen it as a *political* strategy. In this book we are not presenting a blueprint or programme. We try to make a case for the AES as a framework for a viable and progressive strategy, but at the same time set out what we see as the key issues of debate within the AES. The weaknesses that are present in existing formulations should be reason for strengthening the strategy rather than rejecting it.

Although there are many interpretations of the content and objectives of what we refer to as 'the' AES, our case is that it comprises a set of policies which forms a basis for widespread political mobilisation, uniting local and sectional struggles. It is not a strategy that will itself create a socialist society — but it is a strategy that can win tangible gains in the form of jobs and living standards and, perhaps most important, in the form of greater working-class control over production. Moreoever, rather than pursue such gains within the constraints imposed by the existing structure of economic relations, it seeks constantly to anticipate, challenge and progressively dismantle those constraints and substitute new forms of control. Thus we argue that the AES is potentially a progressive and transitional socialist strategy.

## Conclusion

The essential structure of the argument presented in this book can be summed up in a series of key propositions.

1 The crisis we face is both an economic and political crisis which represents an attack on the jobs and living standards of working people and on the organisational strength of the Labour movement.

2 The course of the crisis is not governned by inevitable or mechanical laws: there is an alternative to the present monetarist policies which must be clearly presented.

3 The economic policies of Social Democracy presupposed economic growth, which would reduce class conflict; the Keynes-Beveridge consensus on which post-war politics rested has collapsed and the choices are now more clearly posed.

4 The policies of the Alternative Economic Strategy developed by the Labour movement provide the basis for a viable alternative approach, but they must be debated and developed both economically and politically.

5 It is important to recognise the break in  the working of the economy which would be necessary – the AES would be a break with capitalist forms of economic control and would meet with opposition.

6 The policies of the AES will not create socialism, but are progressive and transitional in the sense that they transform the dynamic of the economy, introducing widespread democratisation and substituting social for market forms of control.

7 It is only through such a transitional economic strategy, which mobilises working people around basic concerns over jobs, living standards, public services and control over our working lives, that progress can be made towards socialism in Britain.

# The Economy in Crisis

## 1. Introduction

Britain has entered a period of profound slump. A slump which promises to be more severe and persistent than the recession of the mid-seventies and which signals a clear break with the economic conditions which allowed relatively stable growth and high employment in the post-war period. Total unemployment has already passed two million and continues to rise; industry is contracting and its profits have collapsed; wages are being forced down below the increase in the cost of living; and public services and welfare benefits are being cut.

If the immediate causes of the economic collapse can be traced to the policies of the Conservative Government, it should be clear that the problems faced are not new. Unemployment remained above one million for the last four years of the last Labour Government, spending plans were drastically cut back in 1975 and 1976, and the Labour movement has for a long time been concerned with the steady decline of industry and slow rate of growth as compared with other countries. In other words we have to understand the current situation in relation to the long term decline of the economy and the growing tensions of the seventies.

Finally it is important to look at the international context. Developments in the UK economy are paralleled to varying degrees in most other capitalist economies and the growing instability of the world economy has interacted with internal factors in generating the current slump.

In the following chapter we will argue that it is useful to understand the current slump as an economic and political crisis which has its origins in the capitalist nature of Britain's economy. We will look at some of the specific factors which have conditioned the development of British capitalism: the extent to which British industry is dominated by large firms, and at Britain's leading role as a base for multi-national companies, the powerful role of the City in influencing economic policy, often against the interests of industrial capital; we look at the defensive strength of the trade union movement, and the declining profitability of industry; and at the relationship between the British and the world economy.

We have to return to some basic questions. Is the process of economic crisis inherent in a capitalist economy? Has the form of government intervention based on Keynes' ideas removed the necessity for the economy to move from boom to slump? Is the British economy still adequately described as a capitalist economy?

By building an understanding of the crisis in this way we can get a much clearer idea of the forces which are conditioning current policy, and the problems an alternative strategy will have to deal with.

## 2. The Dimensions Of The Current Crisis

People experience the economic crisis in different ways. For a growing number, it means redundancy and unemployment, and little prospect of finding employment in the foreseeable future. Others are hit by the decline in the standards of many social services as a result of public expenditure cuts: hospitals and schools have been closed under the camouflage of talk about 'reorganisation'; hopes of people on housing waiting lists have been dashed by the deepest slump in housebuilding since the 1930s. The main factor which determines people's living standards—the real value of their take-home pay—is also coming under increasing threat as unemployment and cash limits are pressing pay settlements to well below the rate of inflation. Let us look at each of these factors more closely.

### *The Collapse of Industry*

Every day we read in the papers of another plant being closed. In 1979/80 such well-known companies as Courtaulds, Singers, Prestcold, British Leyland, Alfred Herbert, British Steel, Massey Ferguson, all closed plants. Company liquidations are at a post-war record level. Industrial output has already fallen sharply and companies are still telling the CBI that they plan further cuts in output and jobs. The high level of the pound—now at its highest level for five years—means that industry has difficulty competing either in export markets or against imports in the home market. In industries like engineering this has meant an enormous drop in orders. It also means a squeeze on the profit margin on this reduced output. The net effect is a fall in the profits of companies to an extremely low level (except for those directly involved in North Sea oil production).

The National Institute of Economic and Social Research has forecast that company profits, excluding those from the North Sea, will fall this year to only 45% of their 1978 level (in real terms) and will drop by a further 10% in 1981. The Cambridge Economic Policy Group, whose pessimism has been amply justified by developments so far, is forecasting that output of the private sector (again excluding oil) in 1985 will be 14% lower than in 1979 if present policies continue.

## Unemployment

In the course of 1980 unemployment is likely to rise by ½ million. It has already set a new post-war record level of around 2 million, or 9% of the labour force. This figure does not include people who are willing to work but do not register as unemployed as they have no incentive to do so—the number of these people is estimated to be in the region of 250,000. Nor does it measure those who would be unemployed but for the various job creation and training schemes recently set up by the government. These are estimated to have kept 235,000 people off the register in early 1980. All the major forecasts show unemployment rising even further in 1981; forecasts for 1982 and beyond are more speculative, but some (the Cambridge Economic Policy Group, the ITEM and the Warwick forecasts) see it reaching 2½ to 3 million in 1982. At present no recovery is in sight: the prospect is for the present slump to deepen, and with it for unemployment to reach numbers similar to those of the worst years of the 1930s.

The general rise in unemployment will not affect the job prospects of all groups of people evenly; for some groups the effects will be particularly severe. There has been and will continue to be an increase in the number of long-term unemployed (those unemployed for a year or more). According to a recent survey (*Dept. of Employment Gazette* January 1980) over three quarters of the long-term unemployed were unskilled people with no formal qualifications. People from ethnic minority groups were also disproportionately represented in the long-term unemployed. There will soon be 2 million people in this category.

Unemployment among school leavers is also at a record level, with one in four school leavers joining the dole queue. Unemployment among older workers has also been increasing particularly fast.

We examine this question further in our chapter on 'getting back to full employment'.

## Cuts in Public Services

The Government has embarked on a determined strategy of cutting back the public sector, which includes selling off public assets, imposing tight financial constraints on nationalised industries and major cuts in public services. In the financial year 1979/80 public spending was cut by £2,000 million compared with Labour's plans, and in 1980/81 it has been cut by £4,000 million. By 1983/84 the Tories plan to reduce the real level of spending to 5 per cent below the level which existed when the Government took office.

Within this shrinking total certain programmes are being expanded – defence is up by 3% a year and social security spending related to unemployment is inevitably rising – while others are being cut back drastically. Housing spending is being cut by 54% over 4 years, regional and general industrial support (including the National Enterprise Board and Regional Development Grants) by 45%, overseas aid by 14% and education by 10%. All these plans are subject to annual 'cash limits' which will force down the real level of services provided if costs – particularly wages – rise faster than the politically determined rate of increase allowed for in the cash limit.

Cuts hit living standards for those who rely on social security benefits for their income, for those who have to pay more for publicly provided goods like transport, energy and housing, and for those who depend on public services for their health and education. They also mean job losses. Cuts hit jobs in four ways: by reducing employment in central and local government; by cutting back on jobs in sectors like construction, which rely heavily on government contracts; by causing redundancies in companies previously supported by government finance; and generally by reducing the level of demand in the economy. As the TUC has emphasised – for every job lost in the public sector another one goes in the private sector.

## Wages and Prices

Meanwhile inflation remains obstinately high. It passed its peak in May 1980 but is likely to remain in the high teens for some time. So far pay settlements have managed to keep up with prices. In the last three years real take-home pay has risen by 8%. The

*12*

situation is in some ways similar to the 1930s where real wages of those in work continued to rise while unemployment stayed over 10%. This situation is unlikely to continue for long into the eighties. Pay settlements will be forced down by a combination of government pressure and unemployment. This is being reinforced by a legal and political attack on trade unions so that their power to resist wage cuts, redundancies and reorganisation of work is weakened.

## 3. The Long-Term Decline

Although the manifestations of economic crisis have become more acute in 1980, with the arrival of a sharp recession, it would be wrong to see the crisis simply as of very recent making, a product of the turbulent seventies. In fact, Britain's economic performance has been weaker than most other industrial countries for the last one hundred years. After its period of dominant ascendancy in the first half of the 19th century, when Britain was the workshop of the world, it lost ground as other capitalist powers emerged. In the mid-19th century it produced about one half of total world manufactures; now it produces about one twentieth. The decline in share has been associated both with a loss of dominance in traditional industries pioneered in the UK, like textiles and mechanical engineering, and with the rise of new industries, all pioneered outside the UK. Chemicals and steel making developed mainly in Germany in the late 19th century, and cars, petrochemicals and computers in the US in the 20th century. The same story could be told of sectors outside manufacturing, such as coal mining and sea transport. The dominance of London as a world financial centre passed to New York, although the relative decline in this respect has been much less pronounced.

We will focus on two areas of long-term decline – the relatively slow growth of living standards and the process of 'deindustrialisation .

### Living Standards

One element of living standards is the value of consumption per head. Although in Britain this has increased over the post-war period, Britain's performance has been much worse than that of any other major capitalist country. In the table below, columns 1 and 2 show an index of real consumption, taking in each case the US=100, in 1955 and 1979.

These figures show firstly that consumption in Britain has declined from 59% to 52% of the US. More significantly, they show the extent to which France, Germany and Japan have improved their relative position, and in the case of the first two substantially over-

Table 2.1:  *Per capita real consumption*

| | 1 | 2 | 3 |
|---|---|---|---|
| | 1955 | 1979 | increase by country 1955-79 |
| | | Index: US=100 | |
| US | 100 | 100 | +80% |
| UK | 59 | 52 | +59% |
| France | 52 | 73 | +154% |
| .Germany | 48 | 67 | +154% |
| Japan | 19 | 48 | +368% |

Source: *OECD Nat. A/C Statistics*
*IMF Yearbook (pop. statistics)*
Beckerman *'Int. Compar. Real Inc.'* OECD, Paris 1966.

taken Britain. Column 3 shows the proportionate increase in real consumption per head of population between 1955 and 1979 for each country. The 59% increase achieved in Britain over 24 years is significant, but is well below the increases in France, Germany and Japan, and below that of the US.

This is a crude indicator, and by no means constitutes an adequate definition of 'living standards'. It excludes those aspects of living standards met through public expenditure. It is also an average figure, and thus does not show the discrepancies between those people and groups with high and those with low consumption. But however crude, it does give a measure of what is widely perceived as an important part of living standards and the extent to which Britain has fallen behind other countries.

## Deindustrialisation

Particularly disturbing is the long run decline of manufacturing industry. In the last 15 years the numbers employed in manufacturing have fallen by 17%, cutting the number of jobs by over 1½ million. The level of production has fallen in the last seven years by more than ten per cent. Meanwhile overseas investment by UK companies has been increasing 2½ times as fast as investment in the UK, which has typically been held down to half or a third the level maintained by our competitors. In Chapter 6 we follow up in more detail the nature and significance of the process of deindustrialisation.

## 4. Developments In The World Economy

The British economy has always been closely integrated into the world economy through trade and finance. The ties have been strengthened more recently by the growing international organisation of industry through multi-nationals; by the extension of international financial markets such as the Eurodollar market; and by the increasing liberalisation of trade, following the moves toward more widespread currency convertibility in the sixties, the negotiation of tariff reductions in the successive rounds of GATT negotiations and the UK's entry to the EEC in 1973. This process of integration has led to far greater coordination of national economic management and has served to harmonise the cycles of activity.

The following table shows trends in inflation, unemployment and economic growth in some of the major capitalist nations.

*Table 2.3: Inflation, unemployment and economic growth in the advanced capitalist countries*

*Inflation in the OECD countries*

Average annual rate of increase of consumer prices, OECD countries.

| | |
|---|---|
| 1961-1970 | 3.4% p.a. |
| 1971-1976 | 8.6% |
| 1977 | 8.7% |
| 1978 | 7.9% |
| 1979 | 9.9% |
| 1980 | 13.5% (March 1979 to March 1980) |

*Unemployment in the EEC countries (the '9')*

Percentage of the labour force registered unemployed in the
nine EEC countries.

| 1970 | 2.0% |
|------|------|
| 1973 | 2.5% |
| 1974 | 2.9% |
| 1975 | 4.3% |
| 1976 | 4.9% |
| 1977 | 5.3% |
| 1978 | 5.5% |
| 1979 | 5.6% |
| 1980 (July) | 5.7% |

*Economic Growth in the EEC countries (the '9')*

| 1970 | 5.0%  p.a. |
|------|------------|
| 1973 | 5.7% |
| 1974 | 1.5% |
| 1975 | 1.4% |
| 1976 | 5.0% |
| 1977 | 2.4% |
| 1978 | 3.1% |
| 1979 | 3.1% |

The figures show that the  signs of a worsening economic
situation have not been confined to Britain. The economic slow-
down has occurred throughout the capitalist world, and has been
accompanied by rising inflation and unemployment. Again the slow-
down has been particularly apparent in industrial production: thus
e.g. industrial production in the EEC countries increased by 83% in
the 1960s but only 23% in the 1970s (these figures are adjusted to
exclude the effect of the enlargement of the EEC in the 1970s). The
figures show too the recessions in 1974-75 and 1980 which were
years of sharp drops in output in Britain. The point then is that
during the 1970s economic conditions have worsened for all
countries that are significantly dependent on trends in world
markets, but as we noted earlier, in these more difficult circumstances the British economy continued to decline relative to the
average of other capitalist countries.

*Financial Instability*

The final collapse of the post-war international financial system that had been set up in 1944 at Bretton Woods came in 1971, when for a period convertibility of the dollar was suspended and the dollar was devalued against other currencies and gold. The fixed exchange rate system was replaced by floating exchange rates, with some of the EEC countries agreeing to restrict the movements of their exchange rates with one another, but sterling and the dollar were left to float. The main factor bringing about the collapse was the massive Balance of Payments deficit of the United States that developed in the late sixties and early seventies, itself a result of the developing relative weakness of the US economy and its resources being overextended in massive overseas investment and military programmes.

The decline in US hegemony left a vacuum in the international monetary system which has not as yet been filled. This has led to greater movements in countries' exchange rates relative to one another and this has exacerbated the world crisis. Exchange rate fluctuations disrupt international trade and discourage investment by increasing risk and uncertainty. A sharp devaluation (such as occurred in Britain in the mid 1970s) increases import prices and gives a sharp upward shift in the inflation spiral which counteracts the effects a devaluation is supposed to have on the adjustment of trade flows. A sharp revaluation (such as occurred in Britain in 1979-80) may have a severe effect on the competitiveness of domestic producers of goods that are internationally traded.

Changes in exchange rates may be necessary and desirable when countries' relative competitiveness is out of line. It is not desirable however for exchange rates to adjust sharply or to fluctuate in response to speculative movements of currency.

Another aspect of this instability is the increase in the volume of funds that are internationally mobile, waiting to switch from one currency into another as individual countries adjust their interest rates, or as expectations about changes in future exchange rates are revised. The growth and spread of multi-national companies have greatly added to this source of instability. Movements of 'hot money' not only respond to, but also cause changes in exchange rates, and this source of instability has increased with the loss of a stable means of storing wealth and the large surpluses earned by the oil-exporting countries.

## The Two Oil Crises

A major factor disrupting the world economy in the seventies was the rise in price of the major energy source of the industrial countries—oil. In a brief period at the end of 1973 and beginning of 1974 the oil producers raised the price of oil fourfold sending shock waves through the consuming countries and radically shifting the balance of world economic power. The price of oil was maintained roughly constant relative to other goods, until the end of 1978 when prices were more than doubled over 18 months.

The increase in oil prices has a number of effects on the world economy. First it effectively redistributes real income from consumers of oil to the producers. As the price of imported oil rises, the reduction in real incomes in the oil-importing countries puts downward pressure on profits and real wages, and this intensifies the struggle within these countries over the distribution of income, which is expressed in the form of rising inflation. Second, it creates imbalances in trade as the producers build up surpluses from the sale of oil which they cannot spend on imported goods. The counterpart of these surpluses are the deficits of importing countries. Third, the oil price rise tends to automatically depress the economies of the importing countries as they find an increasing proportion of spending power drained off into imports.

The response to the first shock centred on the second of these effects and a number of countries reinforced the deflationary effect on their economies trying to cut imports and passing on their deficit to others. Denis Healey, to his credit, was one of the few economic ministers arguing at this time for measures to 'recycle' the OPEC surpluses to remove the need for deflation. Following the second shock, however, the explicit focus for concern has been the first effect—the fall in real income. Policies of deflation by fiscal and monetary means have been widely adopted to try and ensure that it is wages and not profits which bear the brunt of this fall.

## 5. Conclusion

The brief account we have given of the crisis has shown the ways the economy is failing to meet people's needs, both for jobs and an improving standard of living. We have related the immediate 'conjunctural' crisis under the Tory Government to the long term decline of the economy and to the growing instability of the world economy. In the next chapter we attempt to provide a framework for understanding current developments by exploring the concept of crisis as a way in which class conflict is regulated and production reorganised within capitalism. We will also look at certain features of the development of capitalism in Britain which distinguish it from the other major capitalist countries. We cannot hope to give a complete account of the reasons for Britain's current economic situation but we do believe that the factors we identify are the important ones, and are important especially from the point of view of developing an alternative strategy for the economy.

# Understanding the Crisis

## 1. Introduction

In the previous Chapter we described the severe disruption of the economy that is now taking place and the bleak prospects for industry, jobs, living standards and public services in the coming period. We argued that this economic collapse has been precipitated by the actions of the Conservative Government, but that the problems which appear in acute form today are not new. Rather they reflect the outcome of a long term process of structural weakness and relative decline. Moreover, they cannot be separated from the growing instability in the world economy into which Britain is closely integrated. The sharpening of international competition in the current world slump has resulted in particularly severe consequences for the British economy with its relatively weak industrial sector.

In this Chapter we attempt to provide an analysis and explanation of these developments by focussing on the concept of crisis. The term 'crisis' is a sweeping and dramatic one; and its over-use and mis-use threaten to devalue the term, making it a tired and worn cliche, a substitute for concrete argument and analysis. We will try to give the term a clear and precise meaning which in our view makes the concept a valuable tool for understanding what is happening to the economy.

To summarise the argument briefly, we believe that in order to provide a convincing account of economic developments it is essential to recognise that Britain remains a fundamentally capitalist economy. In other words it is a system which operates through markets, in a society divided into classes. By looking at an abstract model of a capitalist system we can see how it is based on continual conflict or struggle within production, over distribution, and between competing capitalists. Periodic crises, or contractions in production, are a characteristic regulatory mechanism in such a system. In other words a crisis is a period of heightened conflict in which the conditions necessary for continued profitable growth are re-established.

In the nineteenth century the regular cycle of boom and slump was clearly evident, but as capitalism has developed, important changes have taken place which have modified the course of crisis. Two crucial changes are the growing concentration of industry and widespread intervention of the state. The effect of concentration is to change the ways in which conflict is expressed and the role of profit, while growing state intervention means that the dynamics of the economy are modified—sudden collapses of production can be avoided, the system can be shored up and the level of demand can be maintained.

These changes led some to argue that the 'mixed economy' created out of state intervention and public ownership had fundamentally transformed the capitalist nature of the economy, and created the possibility of managing the economy to achieve stable full employment and continued growth. As recent experience confirms however, the conflicts underlying the system are not suppressed, but they take different, and increasingly political forms. In particular, conflicts are evident in high levels of inflation and attempts by different governments to regulate the level of wages directly. We use the term 'state managed monopoly capitalism' to describe the economic system of post-war Britain.

This still leaves us without a clear account of the specific problems of the British economy. Our understanding of the capitalist nature of the economy points to a number of important features which should play an important part in accounting for the peculiar course of the economy; the ways we are integrated into the international economy; the dominance of financial interests; the degree of concentration in industry; the strength of the organised Labour movement; and finally the relation of the government to the rest of the economy. By drawing together these features with the concept of crisis as a regulatory mechanism we can grasp the significance of monetarism. Briefly, the current crisis has been precipitated by the Government in a radical attempt to restructure industry and the relations between Capital and Labour by strengthening market forces. It is a crisis in the classic sense.

The purpose of this extended analysis is to provide a basis for assessing the AES. Four important implications which follow are first that the outcome of crisis is not mechanically predetermined, but is the consequence of struggle. Second that the forms of state intervention are crucial in determining the outcome of crisis. Third, that the obstacles to full employment are in a fundamental sense political. Finally, since monetarism represents a radical attempt at economic regulation through markets, any workable alternative must offer effective non-market forms of regulation. In other words our understanding of the causes of the short term crisis and long term decline provides justification for the *possibility* of an alternative strategy for resolving the crisis, and has many implications for the form such a strategy must take. We now turn to spell out these arguments in more detail.

## 2. The Role Of Crisis

Contrary to the views of orthodox economists and most newspaper pundits crisis is not in most cases a sign of mistaken policies or errors in economic management; crises have a vital role to play in the reorganisation of production and in the regulation of the class conflict that is inherent in our economic system. In order to develop this point it is useful to start with an account of a simplified model of our economic system in which the means of production are owned by one class and in which production is organised by exchanging products on unregulated markets.

We will focus on three important features of such a system. The first is that the division of the product into wages and profits will be decided by workers bargaining with capitalists over their money wages. It is significant that 'labour power'—the ability to provide labour—is one commodity which cannot be produced by capitalists, and so supply cannot be expanded at will. As output grows and more labour is needed for production, any surplus of unemployed workers will be depleted and the bargaining strength of those in employment will increase.

This may allow workers to bargain for a larger share of the product going to wages at the expense of profit, and will allow workers to resist attempts by managers to increase profit by raising productivity through increased speed of work and other means. As profit rates decline firms may cut back on investment and some firms may go out of business. At a certain point these growing tensions may precipitate an overall contraction in production—for example a major bankruptcy could lead to a chain of defaults on debt repayments putting suppliers and customers out of business. Through this process the pool of unemployed could be replenished, wages could be forced down, unprofitable producers eliminated and profit rates restored.

The second feature is that the supply of inputs other than labour may also be restricted; particularly if users rely on uncertain supplies from overseas. Shortages and rising prices of raw materials may contribute to the pressures arising from labour shortages. Cotton and wheat would be examples from the nineteenth century, while energy supplies, and particularly the oil price, provide important checks on the smooth process of growth today.

Finally, the fact that production is organised through markets (rather than through barter or through centralised economic planning) means that excess supply in one sector of production relative to the needs of the rest of the economy is signalled by falling prices and profits and more intense competition among producers, possibly leading to bankruptcy.

These three features are useful in explaining the course of economic crisis in nineteenth century Britain. Rising real wages and commodity prices in phases of expansion caused a reduction in profit rates which led to disruptions in supply. Financial commitments, greatly extended in the period of the upswing, could not be met, and creditors, principally banks, would foreclose. Bankruptcies of firms would occur, and even bank failures. The whole credit system would then contract as financial panic set in. Hence a general credit crisis would occur, leading quickly to a general crisis of 'overproduction' as spending fell and firms found themselves with spare production capacity. Unemployment rose and wages fell, laying the basis for a new period of expansion.

This approach suggests a crisis does not herald the necessary final 'collapse' of capitalism. Rather it is a mechanism of regulating the class struggle underlying capitalist production and an outcome of the anarchic conditions of a market economy. As such it is a period of intensification of processes, of struggles, that operate continuously at each stage of capitalist development; struggles by capital to raise productivity, to raise profitability, to eliminate competitors from the market, to gain greater control over the process of production.

## 3. The Growth Of Monopolies And State Intervention

Two important developments require us to modify the simplified account we have given so far and have wide implications for the pattern of economic development. The first is a shift from markets composed of a large number of competing firms to markets dominated by a small number of giant companies. Competition among firms ensures that those firms that do not remain competitive by innovating and cutting costs do not survive. Their markets, and often their assets, will be taken over by the more successful. The result of this process over a long period is a steady concentration of firms into larger and fewer units. Capitalist competition has as its natural result the creation of monopolies. (We use the term monopoly loosely to describe firms which are big enough individually to influence market prices). The UK has been especially prone to this tendency.

The effect of concentration is to give individual firms far greater control over their own destinies. They are no longer subject to a price set in the market, but can set their own prices to give a target rate of profit over and above their costs. Monopoly power means that output (and employment) will primarily depend on the level of demand rather than on the level and rate of profit. A cut in firms' profitability will not necessarily lead to a cut in output so long as the output can be sold at some minimum level of profit, or, temporarily, even sustainable loss. Overproduction therefore arises when the level of demand is insufficient, and not primarily as a result of a fall in profitability. Profitability is to a considerable degree a function of the level of a firm's output.

A second effect of concentration is that firms are able to operate with a substantial cushion of internal finance. This is particularly true of UK firms, 70% of whose finance for investment is internally generated. This may help to insulate firms from the effects of a breakdown in the circuit of credit.

An important consequence of the dominance of the economy by large firms is that profitability tends to *fall* as output contracts. If firms reduce their output they will be operating with surplus capacity so that the cost of producing each unit of output increases. Conversely when the economy expands, unit costs fall and profits tend to rise. If it were not for the effect of expansion in eventually raising wages and other costs, large firms (and small) would be content to see a permanent 'boom'.

The second important development we have to add to our simple model is the enormous extension of state intervention in the economy that has taken place—particularly since the last war. Guided by the economic doctrines associated with the name of Keynes, governments have come to play a far more active role in managing the level of economic activity. By adjusting the level of taxation and public spending and by regulation of credit the government was able to confine economic fluctuations within a narrow margin for nearly three decades. With the development of monopolies, output because more responsive to changes in the level of demand. Keynesian techniques provided the means by which demand could be controlled.

The state is not simply involved in the management of demand. The state at national level may step in to bail out firms in difficulties (e.g. Rolls Royce, British Steel, Volkswagen) though the methods may vary. In all Western capitalist countries one can demonstrate the development of varying forms of permanent or semi-permanent forms of state assistance to firms—for example tax rebates, capital grants, subsidies, and capital reconstruction schemes. This means that a crucial variable determining the financial viability of a company nowadays is net cash flow—the money available to a company from all sources after tax has been paid. Alternatively the state can step in to restructure industry directly using institutions like the Industrial Reorganisation Corporation set up in the 1960s or the National Enterprise Board. Finally the state has been heavily involved in regulating prices and wages and setting the legislative framework within which bargaining between Capital and Labour is conducted.

With its fiscal and monetary instruments that state was able for a time to substitute small recessions for crises; these prevented the erosion of profits becoming too severe. However by removing the basic regulatory function of crisis the state was forced to become even more closely involved in intervening to carry out those processes of regulation directly—in industry and in the labour market.

## 4. The Mixed Economy And The Keynes Beveridge Consensus

We have argued so far that capitalism in post war Britain is significantly different from early capitalism which corresponded more closely to a pure capitalist system. But does this mean that the economy is no longer capitalist?

For much of the period since 1945 there has been a widespread view that the old capitalism, with its periodic crises of unemployment, its inequality and oppression of working people had been changed in some of its fundamentals. There were two main strands to this argument: firstly, that nationalisation of important sectors of industry had created a 'mixed' economy, neither capitalist nor socialist, and that this represented a system in its complete form. And secondly, that state intervention to regulate the economy, to provide a welfare state and to redistribute income had removed the more oppressive aspects of capitalism and reduced the basis for class conflict that had been apparent in earlier times.

The idea that nationalisation simply injects a bit of socialism into capitalism needs to be looked at critically. By and large the state sector in capitalist economies does not compete with private capital, but rather steps in to provide vital services that, for one reason or another, are unprofitable or inefficiently provided through the market. Often nationalised industries have been subordinated to the needs and criteria of the private sector. They have been subject to the gradual introduction of commercial criteria, including a profitability criterion, into their decision-making processes, and have failed to develop participatory forms of management. In short, given the policies that successive governments have obliged the state industries to purse, they have become not staging posts for socialism, but part of the supply lines for capitalism.

What of the case that economic regulation and the welfare state have brought a qualitative change in capitalism?

The essence of what may be called the 'Keynes-Beveridge consensus' is that by certain forms of state intervention, mass unemployment and the oppressive inequalities of earlier capitalism can be reduced or eliminated, while at the same time the principal means of production remain under private ownership and control and are operated to provide profits for their owners. The forms of state intervention involved are what may be described as 'arm's length' intervention: indirect intervention by varying certain very general aggregate quantities such as tax rates, public expenditure levels, interest rates and possibly the exchange rate to create a climate that will stimulate production, investment and employment.

In particular these forms of intervention do not involve changes in the relationship of management and workforce at the point of production: the organisation of work and production remain under the control of management (except in so far as workers are able to use their organised strength to gain some forms of control of their own). Neither do they involve altering the principles of production for the market, that is to let the market and profitability be the arbiter of what should or should not be produced and in what quantity. In both these respects Keynesianism does not seek to replace the two fundamental features of the capitalist system: it does not abolish the classes of workers who sell their labour and owners who control and employ labour for profit; nor does it challenge the role of the market in shaping the pattern of production and employment.

Thus state intervention of this kind could not resolve the basic conflict of interest which remains at the basis of capitalism, the conflict between Labour and Capital over the distribution of income and over the intensity and control of work. As this conflict became intensified by a long period of high employment, by the growing claims of the state and by the inability of the system to meet aspirations for rising living standards, the basis of the consensus collapsed. The rise of monetarism and the attack from the Right on policies of state intervention are a feature of this collapse.

## 5. The Development Of Capitalism In Britain

The argument so far has remained at a fairly general level, and it will, therefore, help to explain the relative decline of the British economy and the severity of the current crisis if we can trace the specific features of the development of British capitalism.

### Industrial Concentration

British industry has a greater concentration of production, investment and employment in large firms than other economies of comparable size and level of development. If we consider for example the very large fims — those with over 40,000 workers — we find there are 30 firms with that number of workers employed in the UK. Those 30 giant firms produced in 1972 35% of all UK manufacturing output. For comparison, no other European country had more than 12 firms of this size operating within its frontiers, and in no case, except the Netherlands, did their share of manufacturing output exceed 20%.

### The Role of Multinationals

As well as having a part of domestic production controlled by giant companies, Britain is also a major home base for multi-national companies, and a major host for overseas based multi-nationals. (A multi-national company — M.N.C. — we define as having substantial production facilities in more than one country). In 1971 the UK was second only to the US as a home base for MNCs — while nearly a fifth of the UK output was produced by overseas based companies. These large firms dominate Britain's trade. Only 108 companies, almost all MNCs, produce half of Britain's exports.

Another way of quantifying multi-nationals is to consider the ratio of the overseas production of MNCs based in a certain country expressed as a proportion of that same country's total production (GDP). This we show below:

*Table 2.2: Overseas production as a % of domestic output 1977*

| Switzerland | 64% |
|---|---|
| UK | 40% |
| Belgium | 25% |
| Netherlands | 23% |
| Sweden | 21% |
| US | 17% |
| Canada | 14% |
| France | 14% |
| Germany | 8% |
| Italy | 7% |
| Japan | 5% |

Source: UNDESA: Multi-nationals Corporation on World Development

With one or two exceptions a league table of post-war economic growth would be an exact inverse of this table. The reasons why low growth is associated with heavy involvement in production in other countries are complex and by no means fully understood. But one general and important reason is that MNCs have a wider horizon than national-based companies when considering plans for production, investment and employment. If there are obstacles to profitable investment in the home country, then rather than tackle those obstacles, they may seek simply to locate overseas. Multi-nationals will often tend to move to the faster-growing economies, and thereby have the effect of reinforcing their growth – and further slowing the growth of production in the slower-growing economies There is evidence that in the 1970s there have been substantial divestments by MNCs operating in the UK (apart from oil). The slow growth, the high inflation, in particular the strong defensive strength of organised Labour in the UK with its high degree of unionisation have caused MNCs to move to countries where wages are lower or productivity greater.

## The Role of the City

The importance of the City of London as a world financial centre has its origin in the pre-industrial period, when Britain's empire and trade were expanding and ever greater amounts of finance were needed for trade and investment, and for growing government (mainly military) expenditure. The City has had a disproportionate influence on the formation of economic policy, with the result that a central aim of policy for a long period was to defend the role of sterling as a key currency in international trade and investment. Thus in 1925, the pound was forced up when Britain went back onto the Gold Standard; in the 1960s, when competitiveness had declined, devaluation was strongly resisted by City interests until the worsening of the trade balance could no longer be suppressed; and again today, when instead of being used to expand the economy the arrival of North Sea oil is being allowed to force up the exchange rate. In each of these situations the maintenance of the strength of sterling is a result of policies which allow the City to flourish as a financial centre while industry loses markets and has its profits squeezed. Even the adherence to free trade and the enthusiasm to join the EEC were reflections of the British role as international financier rather than producer.

The effect of a high exchange rate for MNCs is not as clear-cut as on companies producing at home for export. While the latter suffer a loss of markets and lower profits both in export and the home markets, MNCs derive benefits as well as costs from the sterling appreciation. US companies, for example, operating in the UK find their profits, when converted into dollars, are boosted (this has produced yet another bonanza for the US oil companies with North Sea operations). Sterling appreciation makes it cheaper for UK-based companies to purchase overseas assets (e.g. to buy up foreign-owned companies). The recent expansion of UK investment in the US owes partly to the rise in sterling relative to the dollar. Finally MNCs generally possess the financial resources and expertise to be able to anticipate fluctuations in exchange rates; they have been an important factor in actually causing exchange rate instability by moving large amounts from one currency into another. For MNCs there are benefits, as well as costs, from the appreciation of sterling.

Thus it may be useful to draw a distinction between the interests of financial capital and international industrial capital, which appear to be the main influences on Conservative policy, and the interests of smaller domestic industrial companies on the other hand. The irony of the present Tory Government is that it relies on ideological appeals to small business—the sector which is suffering most heavily from monetarist policies of a high exchange rate and high interest rates.

## *The City and Industry*

As noted above the City has been oriented primarily to overseas activities and to financing the Government. The links between financial and industrial capital have been far weaker than in other countries. Not only has industry relied to a far greater extent on internally generated funds to finance investment than is typical overseas, but the banks and financial institutions have confined themselves more strictly to the role of the rentier capitalist. In contrast to Germany, for example, where the banks play an active role in the management of the companies which they are involved in financing, institutions in Britain have taken an arms length approach to industry. While it is difficult to provide evidence for the direction of causation, the conservatism of the financial institutions toward industry, and the failure to provide long term funds with repayment profiles which correspond to the timing of returns from investments, has certainly reinforced the conservatism and reluctance to take risks evident in industry.

## *North Sea Oil*

In addition to the structural factors reviewed so far we have to include a crucial factor which will condition the pattern of economic development in the eighties and which has had important effects on the way the current crisis has developed—the production of North Sea Oil (NSO). We have now become self sufficient in oil—a dramatic turnaround from the position in 1974 when our net imports of oil equalled nearly 5% of national income.

North Sea oil production provides three kinds of potential benefit to the economy. First there is a direct benefit in jobs and incomes for those employed in the oil sector—probably around 50,000. Second there is a benefit to government revenues from royalties, Petroleum Revenue Tax and the extra Corporation Tax receipts. In 1980 the government share of total NSO revenues will be about one quarter—most of the remainder being profits for the oil companies. It will amount to about £3bn, or 10% of the yield of income tax. This will however rise sharply in the early 1980s: in 1983 the government's share will rise to an estimated 60% or £10bn at 1980 prices. The point is that NSO revenues to the government will soon become a substantial source of revenue, available for tax reductions or increases in public expenditure. The third source of benefit comes from the fact that NSO represents a direct saving of about £8bn on the Balance of Payments: put differently, without NSO and with other things being equal the UK would have a huge Balance of Payments deficit.

Thus NSO production could have been used to relax the Balance of Payments constraints on the economy and allow it to expand, using the revenues to finance expanded public consumption or investment. However, in the context of the deflationary policies pursued in recent years, the contribution of NSO to the Balance of Payments has served only to reinforce the tendency of the pound to rise. By making imports cheaper and exports less competitive abroad this has reinforced the impact of the recession on home production. The result is that under present Tory policies the economic benefits are being distributed as extra consumption. Moreover this is occurring in a highly un-equal way, favouring the better off and penalising others by throwing them onto the dole.

The benefits of NSO could be used to provide valuable resources for a programme of reconstructing the economy and improving the social services; they would make a significant contribution to this end within the framework of an AES.

## 6. Understanding The Current Crisis

We will now try to bring together some of the ideas we have introduced to provide an explanation of the current crisis. It must be stated clearly that the features of the slump, which we have described as constituting a crisis – the massive unemployment, the sharp contraction of industry, the prospects of falling living standards – can be attributed directly to government policy. By combining increases in taxation, substantial public spending cuts, high nominal interest rates, and reductions in support for industry and employment, the government has succeeded in simultaneously contracting demand, increasing costs and restricting credit. The crisis is not due to the world recession; indeed exports have been surprisingly high. Meanwhile (apart from the United States) the UK is the only major country to be suffering an actual contraction of output. Nor can the unemployment be attributed to technological change – the contraction in employment reflects a fall in output, not a rise in productivity. Nor indeed can it be blamed on North Sea oil, which has certainly contributed to the difficulties of manufacturing industry, but only in the context of policies which take as their *objective* a high level of the pound. Each of these factors has contributed to the environment in which government policies have been determined.

We have tried to argue, however, that to understand the origins of the crisis we have to look for the underlying structural constraints which have conditioned the adoption of the monetarist strategy at the present time. Monetarism can be seen as an attempt to restore the force of the market — particularly in the labour market — as an economic and social regulator. The basic conflict underlying capitalism — between Capital and Labour — has expressed itself in the last two decades in the form of falling profit rates and rising inflation. The defensive strength of organised labour in Britain and the fact that major decisions in the economy on production, investment and employment remain very largely under capitalist control, had produced a stalemate. The concentration of industry, the dominance of financial interests, the international orientation of both the City and industry and, more recently, the production of North Sea oil have combined to generate an economy characterised by low investment, low growth in living standards, and a chronically weak industrial base.

This was the situation facing the Labour governments of 1974/79. Although brought to power after a series of industrial confrontations that were won by the trade unions, these governments possessed neither the perspective nor the political resources to bring about a resolution of the stalemate that would permanently subject the economy to greater democratic control and make it more responsive to social needs.

The Tories have attempted to break out of this stalemate and shift the balance of class forces decisively in favour of Capital. They have openly abandoned the postwar 'consensus' with its commitment to full employment and the welfare state. They have made a concerted attack on public expenditure, wages and the organisational strength of the Labour movement, in an attempt to seek a resolution of the crisis which is contingent for its success on the defeat of the trade union movement. By doing so they have raised more sharply for the Labour movement the need to seek a resolution that reflects the needs and interests of working people.

## 7. Implications For Alternative Strategy

The immediate challenge facing the AES is to offer an alternative to the economics of monetarism; a way out which promises higher employment, rising living standards and a new approach to industry. But there is also a more profound challenge; to come to grips with the problem of transforming the economic structures and social relations which have created the long term crisis of the British economy to which monetarism is seen as a solution.

We will end this chapter by drawing out some of the implications for the AES which follow from our analysis. The first is that crisis performs a function within capitalism in resolving or suppressing class conflict and restructuring production. It is a period of heightened struggle and its outcome is therefore subject to contention rather than being the inevitable consequence of a mechanical process. Second, the state has become extensively involved in the management of crisis, at times seeking to stave off a fall in output and taking on the role of social regulation directly, and at others precipitating recession by acting to raise unemployment. Thus, in contrast to some socialists, who see crisis as the occasion to work only to build a socialist consciousness out of the failures of the system, we argue strongly that we have a responsibility to fight as well for alternative policies, different forms of state intervention, which have a significant effect on the outcome of the crisis.

The third point is that the obstacles to full employment are primarily political. We discuss this contention in more detail in Chapters 5 and 11, but it follows from our understanding of conflicts within capitalism that a central contradiction of the system is that the high levels of production and use of resources necessary to maintain profit levels are not compatible with the use of the market to regulate the share of the product going to wages. The demand for full employment, backed up by effective policies is an essentially political demand. Fourth, the reflation of demand, as a basis of an economic strategy for full employment should be effective in increasing output in the short run. The availability of spare capacity means that as demand expands, costs per unit of output would be reduced and profits would rise at least temporarily. Our approach to the current crisis helps to explain why industrialists should back so enthusiastically policies which have decimated industrial profits outside the oil and financial sectors. Clearly it is expected that the long term profits (at least for the companies which survive) from future expansion with a more docile work force and a larger market share for the big companies outweigh the costs currently incurred.

Finally, our approach highlights a fundamental difficulty for the AES. Can the processes of economic regulation be brought under democratic control without the abolition of private capital; a step not envisaged in most presentations? In our discussion of the components of the AES in the following chapters we will defend the position that significant advance is possible through a resolution of the crisis in the interests of the working class, but acknowledge different views as to the instability and the new conflicts engendered by that resolution.

# A Policy for Expansion

## 1. Introduction

The essential basis of any alternative economic strategy must be a policy for planned economic expansion. Without such a policy the prospect of providing higher levels of employment, rising living standards and improved public services would be severely limited. In addition, moves towards a transformation of the social relations and performance of industry would be strictly constrained. A policy for planned expansion would mark a sharp break with the present monetarist strategy, and with the deflationary policies of the previous Labour government. It would be a challenge to the sheer absurdity of a system in which over two million are unemployed while poverty persists, and needs and wants remain unsatisfied; a system in which skills remain unused, and talent and potential are suppressed, and in which vast resources are wasted.

A policy for expansion can be divided into two stages. In the first stage the prime objective would be to bring unused resources into production to provide employment and higher levels of output. In the second stage, once full employment has been reached, further expansion can be achieved only by using resources more efficiently and by employing new techniques of production. There are different problems associated with each stage: in the first an expansion of demand led by the public sector, a 'reflation' of the economy, would play a leading role; in the second stage, different policies would be necessary to guide more rapid expansion. In both stages it is important to ask what it is that we are producing more of, to examine the 'quality' as well as the quantity of growth. We must not lose sight of the fact that capitalist society is based on production of commodities for profit and not production for social need. Since we see the availability of employment as desirable in itself—partly because of the association of employment with social and economic status and partly because of the role unemployment plays as a political regulator—we would see questions of the quality of growth becoming paramount in the second stage. But in the first stage it is extremely important to use the weapons available, particularly the allocation of public spending, to guide the *way* the economy expands. In this chapter we will concentrate on the first stages of expansion.

Is it in fact possible to expand the economy? For years we have been told by leaders of both Parties that 'we cannot spend our way out of unemployment'; we have been assured that we live in the midst of a world crisis whose ineluctable forces we cannot escape; we have been invited to believe that higher unemployment is simply a consequence of the natural progress of technological innovation, of the micro-electronic revolution. We too have argued that we are in the midst of an economic crisis which has roots deep in the soil of British capitalism and which is conditioned by the international integration of the economy. But the key point in our analysis of the crisis is that it is not a mechanical or pre-determined process, but one whose course is determined by class conflict and by state intervention.

It follows that state action can be the starting point—but we emphasise only the starting point—of a strategy aimed at forcing a resolution of the crisis in the interests of the working class. The AES argues clearly that we *can* expand the economy, and that the basis of this expansion should be a reflation of demand led by higher public expenditure and some reduction in taxation for the lower paid. But reflation on its own is quite clearly insufficient—it could well be blocked by a Balance of Payments crisis and a run on the pound, by a collapse of industrial investment and shortages, by fears of rising inflation, by a whole series of other obstacles in which technical difficulties and political obstruction are intertwined. The essence of the AES is that it presents an interlocking set of policies to counter those obstacles and thus ensure a planned and sustained expansion of output.

In this chapter we explain why we regard the broad macro-economic policies of the government as central to any alternative strategy and why we believe that reflation will work. But we go on to look briefly at the obstacles to expansion, and argue that management of demand on its own is inadequate. In the following section we take up the objections to expansion from the Right in both their monetarist' and 'Keynesian' forms, and the objections and criticisms that are made from the Left. Finally we discuss the role of public expenditure in the AES, arguing that it must play a central role.

Campaigns against cuts in spending, if they are not to be dissipated, ·must become campaigns for an alternative economic strategy which can provide *increased* spending under far greater democratic control. A crucial organising focus for policies of expansion is the objective of restoring full employment. We turn to the question of unemployment in Chapter 6 discussing the question whether expanding output is sufficient to create the jobs we need.

## 2. The Case For Expansion Through Structured Reflation

We have argued that the basis of the first stage of a policy for expansion should be a reflation of the economy—a reflation of demand led by the public sector. To justify this claim it is worth outlining certain simple ideas about the way the economy works which have in recent years been displaced by the fashionable sophistication of monetarism. The ideas are associated with the name of Keynes but they are by no means a complete account of his views. Nor do they give a comprehensive account of the working of the economy Their significance is that they were developed in opposition to the economic orthodoxy of the twenties and thirties which is now reproduced in the new depression of the eighties in the guise of monetarism. Briefly they argue that the level of employment is not independently determined by market forces beyond control, but can and should be influenced by governments to maintain a high level of employment. In other words in rejecting monetarist deflation we want to rescue certain basic ideas from Keynesianism which we see as extremely valuable for the Labour government, and integrate them into our new approach.

A useful place to start is with the circular flow of income. We can see clearly in Britain at the moment a process of cumulative decline. A cut in public spending means among other things that fewer construction workers, teachers or nurses are employed. One effect of this is a fall in demand for consumer goods such as cars, so car workers are laid off as unsold stocks build up, and their spending is cut back. Meanwhile demand for car components and steel is reduced, so that these industries contract, leading to reduced demand for coking coal for blast furnaces. This means that pits are closed and miners join steel workers, engineers, car workers and teachers in the dole queue, all contributing to a fall in spending and a fall in tax revenues. And then the government tells us that public spending must be cut further to cut public borrowing and balance the budget because 'as every housewife knows' you cannot spend more than you earn. As Keynes remarked, this process may well end up with a balanced budget—at zero on both sides.

The simple idea of reflation is to reverse this process, turning it into one of cumulative expansion. An initial stimulus from increased public spending, cuts in tax or an expansion of credit will raise incomes and these incomes in turn will be spent creating a further expansion of demand. This process is known as the 'multiplier' effect. Cumulative expansion does not continue indefinitely because the process is clearly by no means as smooth as we have portrayed it so far. First, a certain proportion of additional incomes will go in income tax and savings rather than being spent—generally, the higher the income the less is spent. Second a proportion of spending will not go to create new incomes in this country, either because it is lost in taxes on spending or spent on goods from overseas. Savings, taxation and imports are said to be 'leakages' from the circular flow of income and reduce the impact of any initial stimulus.

Two further potential obstacles must be noted. The first is that any initial stimulus must be financed in some way. Public spending over and above that financed by taxation must be paid for by borrowing or by credit expansion. In the first case it could be argued that lending to the government cuts spending in other areas while monetarists argue that credit expansion simply causes inflation. The second potential obstacle is that for a variety of reasons firms may respond to additional demand not by raising their output but by raising the price of their goods. We return to these difficulties below.

Does it matter how the government reflates the economy? We have mentioned the possibility of using tax or spending policy (fiscal policy) or credit expansion (monetary policy). There are clear advantages in using spending policy, first because it would allow rapid moves towards reversing cuts made by the Tories, and would allow greater control over the areas in which output was expanding. Within public expenditure there is a spectrum ranging from those kinds of spending where the government determines the pattern (as with a decision to build a new hospital or nuclear submarine) through to transfers of spending power to individuals over which the government then has no control (as with pensions or social security payments). The nearer we are to the beginning of this spectrum, the more control the government has over the pattern of expansion. Second, spending is far more effective than tax cuts in creating jobs and expansion, because part of any tax cut will go on savings and imports, while a large part of public spending will go directly on labour-intensive services. However spending plans take some time to put into effect, so there would be a good case for stimulating expansion in the short run by tax cuts for the lower paid which takes immediate effect, and for drawing up public sector projects in advance which could be rapidly implemented. Thus we would argue for a carefully structured reflation based on increased public spending but with some tax reductions as an initial injection of demand.

To argue simply for reflation however is obviously insufficient without steps to overcome the obstacles to expansion mentioned earlier. We give a brief account of each of these obstacles here in order to show how the AES ties together the measures which would be necessary to support sustained expansion. The first problem is that as demand expands substantial proportion of the additional demand created would be spent on goods from overseas, and experience suggests that a very substantial devaluation of the pound would be necessary to counteract this pressure. The result would be that imports would soon outweigh exports, and the consequent Balance of Payments deficit may spark a run on the pound and a sterling crisis, as has happened so often in the past. The likelihood is that this difficulty would not be removed by North Sea oil production. Thus we argue in Chapters 9 and 10 below that it would be necessary to take steps to plan and limit the growth in imports directly and to control international capital movements.

The second obstacle is that a rapid expansion of demand may not induce an expansion of production if there are 'supply bottlenecks' arising for example from the delay before unused capacity can be brought into production, new production lines can be tooled-up, or workers can be re-employed and trained. This problem may be particularly severe in the aftermath of the Thatcher government when industrial production will have been substantially reduced and domestic capacity in certain sectors virtually eliminated. This kind of difficulty can be met by controlling the rate of expansion, and directing public sector demand to those areas which can be most easily expanded in the short run while a system of industrial planning is being established. We discuss the industrial strategy which is an integral part of the AES in Chapter 6. A particular form of supply constraint—the availability of skilled labour—requires active intervention in the labour market to develop a comprehensive manpower policy. This is taken up in the following chapter.

Third, in an expanding economy and particularly after a period in which real wages have been depressed, there is a serious danger of inflation rising as firms take advantage of tight markets to raise profit margins while workers seek to restore differentials and relativities eroded in the recession or distorted by the current discrimination against the public sector. To limit the danger of inflation leading to a break-down of the strategy we argue that the AES should include a clear programme for controlling inflation based on price controls and an agreement on income determination. We explore this field in Chapter 10.

Finally, reflation will, at least in the short run, increase the amount the government has to borrow (the Public Sector Borrowing Requirement PSBR). We do not see this as a problem in any real sense, but there may be a need to increase sales of government debt. The last Labour Government made a great deal of their claim that borrowing could not be increased because the institutions of the City would not finance it. Although we regard this claim as exaggerated it would seem sensible to take measures to reduce any hold the City may have over determination of economic policy. We return to the question of public sector borrowing below.

Thus in this section we have argued the simple case for reflation as the basis for expansion, but made clear that to stand a chance of success reflation must be buttressed by a series of supporting policies covering trade, capital movements, industry, employment, prices and the financial system. It is these interlinking measures which give the AES its coherence as a programme for planned expansion.

## 3. The Opposition To A Policy For Expansion

The basic ideas outlined above have come under sustained attack from the Right. Both monetarists and non-monetarists have made the case that it is simply not possible to expand the economy by reflating, but that it is necessary to cut public spending and reduce public sector borrowing. It is a tragedy that such ideas should have gained credence in sections of the Labour movement; it is important that they be openly contested. In this section we go into the theoretical basis of such ideas in order to show that they are deeply flawed at an analytical level. However this technical debate is ultimately of secondary importance because, as we have argued, the fundamental obstacles to full employment under capitalism are political—at full employment the market loses its force as a system of social regulation.

Monetarism is not just a theory of inflation. It is a series of propositions stating that fiscal policy is useless, that all economic management is counterproductive, that all unemployment is voluntary, and that economic welfare is maximised by giving the greatest possible freedom to the operation of market forces. These propositions are embedded in a political and economic philosophy which is profoundly hostile to the public sector and deeply reactionary in its implications. It is the ideology of market capitalism par excellence.

Monetarists have argued that there is a 'natural rate' of unemployment to which the economy would tend if left to the free operation of market forces. Governments, it is argued, can only influence the level of unemployment by influencing the expectations of people looking for work, so that they think the real wages they will be paid are higher than they turn out to be. The way they can influence expectations is by increasing the money supply which leads to an increase in spending, so bidding up the price of labour as firms seek to create a sellers' market in which more goods will be sold, while their prices are bid upwards. As profit margins increase firms are induced to take on more labour, reducing unemployment and causing money wages to edge up. Because the pressure of an increase in money supply is first of all on the prices of goods and services, it will cause real wages to fall. It is, say the monetarists, this fall in real wages that permits employment to increase. But, they argue, when the fall has been fully perceived by workers they will reduce their supply of labour until money wages rise sufficiently to restore real wages. As real wages rise, employment falls: the net result is no change in employment, but higher inflation.

In other words the government can bring unemployment temporarily below the natural rate by monetary expansion, but any attempt to keep it below will require accelerating monetary expansion and thus accelerating inflation. Thus the 'real' economy operates independently of the 'monetary' economy except when the expectations of the actors in the real economy are changed, and the main factor determining these expectations is the growth in the money supply. Finally it is argued that fiscal policy is ineffective because any increase in public spending financed by borrowing reduces private spending by a corresponding amount – there is complete 'crowding out' of private spending.

The outcome of this rather implausible story is that monetarists argue that it is futile to try to expand the economy to increase output and employment. Tax and spending policy make no difference except to the extent that taxation reduces incentives, while monetary policy only produces temporary benefits in output at the expense of higher inflation. It is precisely this line of argument which was echoed by Mr. Callaghan in his famous statement to the Labour Party Conference when he said:

"We used to think that you could spend your way out of a recession, and increase employment by cutting taxes and boosting government spending. I tell you in all candour that that option no longer exists, and that in so far as it ever did exist, it only worked . . .by injecting a bigger dose of inflation into the system."

Statements of this kind were often backed up with the assertion that we have to defeat inflation first before we can expand. Although Mr Callaghan would almost certainly not subscribe to the theoretical baggage of monetarism, and we would not underplay the important changes between the economic policy of this Tory government and the last Labour administration, in practical terms his rejection of expansion was very similar to that offered by monetarism. Sufficiently similar, in fact, to ensure that the Tories can deflate any Opposition attack by simply quoting back earlier speeches by the Labour Party leadership.

Unfortunately there is not the space to provide a comprehensive criticism of this rejection of reflation here. We will focus on one question which has been the centre of attention—the size of the PSBR—because it underlies the cuts in public spending over the last five years. Monetarists and non-monetarists have argued that the level of government borrowing has been excessive and damaging because it has 'crowded out' productive investment in the private sector by reducing the availability of finance, and by increasing its price (the rate of interest). Furthermore, any borrowing that cannot be financed from the private sector contributes to monetary expansion which is seen as causing inflation. Monetarists have backed this up with homilies about thrift and the fact that the government, like any household, cannot 'live beyond its means'. Borrowing can be cut by reducing spending or increasing taxation; the monetarist attack on the public sector makes certain that it is spending which goes.

In opposition to this line of thinking it is important to argue first that it is perfectly legitimate for the government to borrow. Just as any sensible household would borrow to make a major purchase or any company would borrow to finance its investment, it makes sense for the government—which undertakes over 40% of all investment in the economy—to borrow.

This is particularly true when we remember that the PSBR includes the borrowing of nationalised industries. Moreover, in a capitalist economy savings decisions and investment decisions, as

Keynes pointed out, are unlikely to match each other. If the savings of one group are not matched by investment elsewhere, output will go unsold and the economy will go into recession. Thus even in a capitalist economy it makes sense for the government to borrow and spend surplus savings in the economy if the aim is to prevent a recession occurring.

A third justification for borrowing is that the level of borrowing varies automatically with the level of activity in the economy. As unemployment rises, spending on benefits rise while tax revenues fall It is estimated that the cost to the exchequer of keeping a married man with two children unemployed is roughly equivalent to the average level of earnings—something like £6,000 a year. This is why borrowing is tending to rise at present and why the government is forced into new cuts to keep it down. It is also why borrowing may well *fall* as output expands under reflation. Finally the nature of the 'burden' of debt in times of inflation is often misrepresented. You would not guess from the propaganda about the overwhelming burden of debt, that the National Debt currently outstanding is at its lowest point in relation to output for nearly two hundred years. This is largely due to the impact of inflation which erodes the real value of outstanding debt and ensures that (as long as the rate of inflation exceeds the rate of interest) the government is actually being *paid* to borrow money—it pays back less than it borrows.

For all these reasons we would argue that a high level of borrowing to finance reflation is clearly justified in economic terms. Moreover the monetarist case against the PSBR is largely fabricated. It is nonsense to suggest that cuts are necessary to prevent 'crowding out' because (as the Government and City are very keen to tell us when arguing against any changes in the financial system) there really is no shortage of funds. Even if there were, it is by no means obvious that the private sector would use them any more productively than the government. There is, furthermore, no evidence of a correlation between the PSBR and money supply. Over the last ten years the correlation between these variables has been precisely zero. But the existence of a correlation would be no objection to borrowing, since an expansion of credit would contribute to reflation of demand. There is no reason why public borrowing financed by credit expansion should be more inflationary than corresponding degree of reflation achieved by other means.

Briefly then we reject the monetarist and Right-Keynesian attacks on reflation and the case they make for public spending cuts.

Although we have argued on technical grounds, we see the arguments as the expression of underlying political conflicts. Monetarism seeks to restore the role of the market as a social regulator.

## 4. Some Criticisms From The Left

In this section we take up two responses from the Left to a proposal for a strategy based on reflation.

The first is that it is simply traditional Keynesianism designed to regulate capitalism rather than provide impetus to a transition towards socialism. The second is that it sounds fine but it simply won't work. The cause of the crisis is the falling rate of profit and it is futile to hope that capitalist enterprises will expand their output without an increase in profits.

Our reply to the first point is that the value of any demand depends on its context—for us what is important about the AES is that it advances a case for reflation within a framework of a strategy the components of which are mutually reinforcing. Thus, rather than accepting and working within the usual constraints on policy imposed by the need to maintain the system of profit, the AES presents a direct challenge to those constraints. To ensure that a move towards full employment initiated by reflation can be sustained it is necessary to introduce policies for the control of trade and prices and the planning of industry.

But we have no illusions that this is simply a technical construction—an alternative set of policies to be adopted by the state. The interplay of political and economic forces ensures that the success of the strategy is contingent on political mobilisation to achieve democratic control over industry, over public spending and over the administration of public services. The AES presents a flexible dynamic strategy to counter the dynamics of the capitalist economy.

The second objection concerning profitability can be presented in different ways, but what it amounts to is this: that the function of the crisis is to force down real wages, to reinforce management control of production and eliminate inefficient producers so that future expansion can take place on a profitable basis. The AES, by refusing to allow this process to take place, offers no prospect of expansion without the wholesale replacement of capitalist production. Businesses may be unable to compete with competitors overseas which have been more effectively restructured on a capitalist basis. Alternatively the trade unions may be in a sufficiently strong position to press wage claims which could initiate an inflationary spiral or could eliminate profit and thus make the privately-owned sector non-viable.

It might be argued that as the economy expands firms' productive capacity will be used at higher and more efficient levels of production so that unit costs would be reduced and profits would increase. Profit levels do tend to rise in the expansion phase of the business cycle and so an initial reflation would be likely to lead to expanded production in the private sector. But we have also argued that as a higher level of output is sustained for a period the bargaining power of labour increases and rising wages then force down profits. After a period of reflation then a 'profit crisis' would develop. Would this matter?

As we argue in Chapter 6 an essential part of the industrial strategy is to reduce the role of profit in the economy, both as a source of funds to finance investment and as the criterion that determines where investments should or should not be made. The AES aims to replace the form of restructuring that takes place through recession by developing new democratic processes for planning the development and structure of industry. These processes would be backed up by real powers over the allocation of investment funds by workers' organisations. The point to emphasise is that if we are to have sustained full employment we must also develop new social mechanisms for the restructuring and adaptation of industry. This is yet another way in which the elements of the AES are interconnected.

In considering the challenge of developing these new mechanisms we should not lose sight of the fact that the present system of restructuring through slump and the market is enormously costly in terms of lost output, and that the burden falls always and wholly upon the working class.

## 5 Public Expenditure and Expansion

It is often through change in the level of public spending that economic decisions have their most immediate effect on people's lives. For example, workers in the public sector who have lost their jobs or whose wages have been held down by cash limits, or those who use and depend on public services, are confronted directly with arguments about the appropriate level of public expenditure. The cuts made by the last two governments have generated considerable opposition and led to the formation of many campaigns to defend services – some of which have had successes but many of which have had little or no impact. There are some important lessons to be learnt from these campaigns for building support for an AES.

The first lesson is that decisions made centrally are the crucial determinant in the level of spending. About 25% of public spending is undertaken by local rather than central government, but 60% of this spending is financed by grants from central government (the rate support grant) and only 40% is financed locally out of rates and charges under local authority control. Capital spending financed by borrowing is mostly under central control. The rate support grant is fixed as a proportion of the amount that central government has planned for local government to spend and is reinforced by a cash limit. Local authorities, then, can oppose cuts but at a price; rates and charges have to be increased by some 2½% for every 1% the authority is spending over the government's plans. Area Health Authorities which are responsible for making spending decisions in the Health Service are even further constrained by having no power to raise revenue.

In other words responsibility for cuts is devolved while power is centralised, and so no government committed to cuts is going to be too troubled by opposition directed against those who are being forced to implement the decisions it has imposed.

Various strategies have been discussed to fight this dilemma including defaulting on debt charges, refusing to cut or raise rates and so forcing rapid insolvency, or mass resignation of councillors. The worth of such gestures would be entirely dependent on the kind of political campaign within which they were carried out, but unless they succeeded in either bringing down the government or reversing its entire strategy (both highly unlikely) they would be merely expressions of impotence rather than demonstrations of strength. Thus the kind of economic strategy pursued by the central government does have crucial effects which no one on the Left can afford to ignore.

The second lesson which follows from the first is that there is a serious danger that campaigns against cuts simply become divisive. As long as the overall level of spending is fixed by cash limit and other measures, a successful struggle against cuts or closures in one field may simply lead to cuts being transferred to fields in which opposition is less well organised. This is in no way to suggest that such campaigns should not be organised—their role in involving people in political issues is invaluable in itself—but rather that without a perspective of controlling and increasing the *overall* level of spending such campaigns could turn from a source of solidarity into a force of disunity and disillusion.

The third point is that in organising opposition to cuts it is not enough to make clear the need for services, we also have to show how they can be paid for. We have to take on the arguments for cuts directly, as we have tried to do above, and make a clear case for higher public spending, but with far greater democracy in the alloc- ation of spending and the provision of services. We have to show how the economy can be organised differently so as to provide growing resources for the public sector.

In short, we have to move from the defensive to make a positive case for public spending. Public expenditure is vital for four quite different reasons. *First* it serves to raise the level of demand in the economy. Whether spending is on nurses' wages, the expenses of building a new school or higher pensions, it feeds into the rest of the economy as wages or pensions are spent or construction workers are employed. In other words spending goes to provide jobs right thrgough the economy as it contributes to the circular flow of income. *Second* public expenditure on the wages of public sector workers provides jobs directly in the public sector. This is very important because we cannot expect industry to create many extra jobs because of the speed of technical change and job-saving invest- ment. The expansion of employment will have to come in services. *Third* public spending enables public services to be improved and so makes a major contribution to our living standards. It has the extra advantage of distributing benefits far more equally than private incomes so it contributes to greater equality. Finally public spending is important because it is a challenge to the market, a challenge to the determination of priorities by the dictates of private profitabil- ity. Through public spending and the democratic planning process outlined below we can develop a new idea of what prosperity is and what the goals of economic growth are.

But how can public expenditure be paid for? In the first stage of expansion higher spending will initially be paid for out of borrowing together with a redirection of revenues from North Sea oil. To some extent spending at this stage will pay for itself, as unemploy- ment is reduced so cutting social security spending and increasing tax revenue. In the second stage however, once resources are fully used higher spending will largely have to come either as a result of economic growth or by raising tax rates. Some revenue can be raised through the surpluses of new nationalised industries. More revenue should be raised through corporation tax and capital taxes, but we should not delude ourselves that these sources can finance the com- prehensive programme of social reforms we would like to see imple- mented. As socialists we should not shy away from arguing for fair collective payment through tax for collective provision of services.

## 6. Conclusion

In this chapter we have argued for a policy of expansion based on planned reflation of the economy as the framework for an alternative strategy. A higher level of public expenditure would be an important part of the reflation, and campaigns against spending cuts, if they are not to be dissipated, must be linked to the case for a broad strategy for expansion. Reflation on its own however would face many obstacles without a series of accompanying policies which are integral to the AES. These policies would help to oversome the technical obstacles to reflation leaving the political opposition to full employment, which underlies opposition from the Right, more clearly exposed.

# Getting back to
# Full Employment

## 1. Introduction

The crisis of unemployment will be the key issue of the eighties. The number of unemployed is the central manifestation of the economic crisis and any alternative strategy for resolving the crisis must offer some prospect of moving the economy back to full employment. In the previous chapter we argued for a policy of expansion designed to provide jobs, rising living standards and improved public services. In this chapter we take up the question of employment in more detail, justifying our claim that the growth of output is crucial in determining the level of employment and looking at the debates over the impact of new technology and the possibility of permanent structural unemployment. We then go on to discuss different approaches to reduce unemployment through reduced working time, through setting up special employment and training programmes and through workers' plans of production as an alternative to redundancy. We argue that all these should play a part within an overall economic strategy, but that they would have little impact if seen as *substitutes* for an AES.

Before turning to these issues it is worth spelling out why we see full employment as a central objective. Not only has a certain fatalism crept into thinking on the subject, but it is sometimes associated with complacency. On the Right this may be supported by theories that all unemployment is really voluntary and has been encouraged by high levels of welfare benefits – despite all the evidence to the contrary. On the Left, some take the view that unemployment should be welcomed as an escape from work under the alienating conditions of capitalist production. We reject both these positions, first because it should be absolutely clear that variations in the level of employment have very little to do with choice – it would be absurd to suggest that unemployment is rising at the moment because more people have decided that they prefer

*49*

the dole queue. Second it would be quite wrong to understate the costs borne by the unemployed—the loss of income, loss of skills, loss of status, or the hardship, strain and humiliation suffered by those thrown out of work or those who leave school and are unable to get work. Finally, higher unemployment is not just a problem for the unemployed. It is a threat to the job security of everyone and so undermines effective trade union organisation and weakens bargaining strength.

It is in this sense that unemployment is an instrument of social regulation. Measures to raise unemployment such as those adopted by the Tories are attempts to strengthen the operation of market forces in the labour market at the expense of working-class living attempt to reverse this process and assert the collective strength of the Labour movement. That is why it is central to the AES.

## 2 Dimensions Of The Jobs Crisis

The latest available figures at the time of writing (July 1980) show total registered unemployment of just under 1.9 million in the UK, with the seasonally adjusted figures for adults at 1.6 million. These figures will undoubtedly rise, yet even they do not reveal the true extent of unemployment. Moreover particular groups and regions will be worse hit than others; the impact of the crisis is uneven.

The average level of adult unemployment in the UK in the 1950s was 332,000 and in the 1960s the level rose to 447,000. In the first half of the seventies the figure rose by over 50% to 689,000 and in the second half it nearly doubled to 1,251,000. It is generally expected that the level of adult unemployment will rise to close on two million by early 1981, and most forecasters expect the trend to upwards after that for at least two years. The Cambridge Economic Policy Group has been among the most pessimistic forecasters, suggesting that if present policies continue unemployment could rise to as much as 4½ million by 1985. There is no doubt that without a drastic reversal in the strategy of the present Government we will be faced with a return to levels of mass unemployment not seen since the early 1930s, when the numbers out of work reached nearly 3 million. Unemployment is obviously not confined to this country. There are over 6 million unemployed in the EEC and over 20 million in the 24 main industrial countries of the OECD.

The figures for those registered as unemployed do not, however, take into account the 'hidden' unemployment that exists. First there are a number of groups registered but not included in the count. One is those who are not claiming unemployment benefit and only seeking part-time work. At the end of 1979 there were 36,000 of these, 95% of whom were women. A second group comprises those who are laid off or 'temporarily stopped' by their employers—an average of 12,000 through 1979. Third there are adult students looking for vacation work, a figure of over 120,000 in September.

There is also a much larger group of people who regard themselves as looking for work but are not registered, often because they would not be entitled to any kind of benefit. The Department of Employment estimates that this group numbers 300-350,000, three-quarters of whom are women. Finally there may be far greater numbers of people, particularly women, who are not looking for work but who would happily take up jobs if they were available with the right hours and pay. This group by its nature cannot be measured but it means that as employment expands not everyone taking up work is coming off the register. In short, the real level of unemployment in mid-1980 is probably nearer 2½ million than 1.9 million. In addition there are about 350,000 jobs and training places supported by special schemes such as the 'Temporary Short Time Working Compensation Scheme' and the 'Youth Opportunities Programme'. These schemes are probably keeping over 200,000 people off the register at the moment.

We can indicate how the jobs crisis has hit certain groups particularly hard—school leavers, blacks, women and people in certain regions. There will be a generally high level of young people coming into the labour force over the next few years which, in the current depression, means a rapidly growing level of youth unemployment. A recent forecast by the Manpower Services Commission predicted that the average level of unemployment among school leavers would rise from 92,000 in 1979 to 214,000 in 1982, while the number of unemployed people under the age of 19 would go up by nearly 90% from 254,000 in 1979 to 478,000 in 1982. (These figures do not take into account special training measures which occupied 60,000 school leavers last year.)

It is difficult to find systematic evidence of higher unemployment rates in the black community although local experience suggests that discrimination intensifies as unemployment rises. The Department of Employment publishes figures for unemployment among 'minority group' workers which show that while unemployment in the UK grew by 16% in the year to May 1980, unemployment in minority groups rose by 26%. The figures also suggest that women are more likely than men to lose their jobs. Over the same period unemployment amongst women rose by 22% as compared with a 14% rise for men.

The regional pattern of unemployment is highly uneven. The percentage of the labour force out of work varies from 12% in Northern Ireland and 10% in the Northern region down to 4% in London and the South-East. These regional figures mask even greater local disparities. Unemployment on Merseyside is at 13% and, in North-East Wales, over 14%.

## 3. Expansion and Employment

In the previous section we have tried to document the seriousness of the crisis and its uneven impact. We have made clear that we see unemployment as an indication of the contradictions and failures of a particular form of economic organisation and management; it is in no sense inevitable. Thus we reject defeatist views about unemployment, and would argue that the demand for full employment to be restored within a five-year period should be a central organising focus of the AES.

Can such a target be achieved? We believe that through the measures outlined in the previous chapter to expand the economy, despite the numerous obstacles, full employment can be restored. To indicate what the target means in terms of jobs we can make a few simple assumptions. In setting the level of full employment precise definitions are less important than targets. A reasonable full employment target would be to have no more than 2½% of the labour force out of work, a level of unemployment of 650,000. This could obviously be revised once it had been achieved. Second, if we assume that the level of unemployment in the circumstances of an AES being implemented could be in the region of 2¼ million, then we would be seeking a reduction in the number of registered unemployed of 1.6 million. Third, if past relationships continue, it would be necessary to create ten jobs for every six people taken off the register, because some jobs would be taken by people who were not registered as unemployed. Finally it would be necessary to create an additional 0.8 million jobs to take account of the increase in the labour force over a five-year period.

In short, to restore full employment it would be necessary to create nearly 3½ million jobs over a five-year period, or 700,000 extra jobs a year. A daunting prospect, but an objective by no means impossible to achieve. To provide an increase in the number of jobs available on this scale would require an increase in the level of employment of about 2¾% a year. If there was no change in the relation between employment and output, this could be achieved by an expansion in output of this amount. However we could expect productivity – output per worker – to increase, perhaps by about 2% a year over a five-year period under normal circumstances. In addition the introduction of new micro-electronic technology may add around 1% to productivity growth. Taking these figures together we find that on fairly plausible assumptions a growth rate of output of around 5¾% a year would be necessary to restore full employment in five years.

The one variable we have not yet taken into account is the time spent at work. If we could achieve a 1½% reduction in weekly hours worked – bringing the average down from its present level of 41.5 hours to 38.5 hours – then our required growth rate would be adjusted downwards to just over 4% a year. Growth at this level, we would argue, is well within our capability.

*Table 5.1: Growth of employment and output required to restore restore full employment in a period of five years*

*Growth in employment required:*

| | |
|---|---|
| Reduction in registered unemployment to 0.65m | 1.6 million |
| Reduction in unregistered unemployment | 1.0 million |
| Increase in the labour force | 0.8 million |
| Total increase in employment required | 3.4 million |

*Economic growth required:*

| | |
|---|---|
| Basic (equal to the annual growth in employment required) | 2.7% p.a. |
| Plus growth in productivity | 2.0 |
| Additional productivity growth due to new technology | 1.0 |
| Less reduction in working time | −1.5 |
| *Annual growth in output required* | 4.2% p.a. |

We have set out the simple arithmetic of full employment, based on plausible assumptions about the relevant factors, to try to dispel the idea that full employment is a goal beyond our reach. In doing so we have made a number of necessary simplifications which will be qualified below. At this stage it is worth noting two points about the distribution of employment. *First, the impact on employment is crucially dependent on the way the economy expands.* Generally expansion initiated by public expenditure increases generates a far greater number of jobs than an equivalent stimulus provided by tax cuts. Simulations with the Treasury model found that an injection of £1,000 million (at 1977 prices) through increased public spending resulted in an additional 260,000 jobs being created after two years, nearly four times as many as a resulted from a corresponding stimulus provided by cuts in income tax. The job-creating impact of expansion led by public spending can be further enhanced by concentrating spending in labour-intensive services, and initiating new programmes such as compulsory home insulation.

The second point is that little additional employment can be expected in manufacturing industry. From past experience it is likely that manufacturing will meet additional demand by using capacity more efficiently without substantial changes in its labour force. Additional jobs will come primarily in public and private services and in construction. One particular myth, which has recently been fostered by the Tories and has gained some credence, is that within manufacturing it is new small firms which will be the main source of new jobs. One piece of evidence often quoted in support of this idea is the report by David Birch on job creation in the United States. This report found that 66% of net new jobs that were created were in firms with less than 20 employees. It is important to note however that this study covered service as well as manufacturing, and that a large contribution by small firms to *net* new jobs tells us nothing about their contribution to total new jobs created or about their role in the overall process of job creation and destruction. In other words we should be wary of attempts to cultivate the ideology of the small firm which can simply be a smokescreen for policies which are doing immense damage to industry as a whole.

## 4. The Impact Of New Technology

To many it may appear that we have taken an optimistic view about the possibility of high levels of unemployment. It may be objected that we have underestimated the employment effects which will follow from the introduction of new technology based on micro-electronics—the 'silicon chip'. Revolutionary technological changes of this kind have many implications—for the pattern of employment, for the balance of skills needed in the labour force, for the control of the production process, and for the nature of work people are required to perform.

The trade union movement has been justifiably concerned, and has led the way in raising these issues and encouraging debate on the economic and social consequences of new technology. We should, however, try to put the employment effects of technology in perspective, and in particular, we would argue that we should not accept ideas of permanent technological unemployment. Labour-saving innovations have been introduced continuously throughout the history of capitalism and there is no evidence that micro-electronics will initiate a structural change in this process on the scale that many have speculated. In the US for example where the introduction of this particular technology is far advanced, employment rose by some 10 million in the two years after 1975. Even though the situation is not strictly comparable it illustrates the possibility of exaggerating the scale of job loss. Moreover, even on the most pessimistic assumptions, for example those of Barron and Curnow, it is estimated that new technology will displace some 4 million jobs over the next 15 years. This figure is equivalent to a rise in productivity of 1% a year, which can be compared with an average rise in productivity of 2% over the last 20 years.

In short the introduction of new technology in an unplanned way and in an economy which was not expanding would certainly make the prospects for employment much worse. But in a co-ordinated strategy for expansion linked to industrial planning and with some reduction in working time, there is no reason why the use of micro-electronics should not be compatible with a return to full employment. It is all too useful for governments to be able to blame unemployment on the impersonal forces of technical change—the Labour movement should not be distracted by this.

But we cannot accept the proposition that rapid technological change will in some way benefit working people automatically. Rather it is a field for struggle. First, although the overall level of employment may be rising, there may well be serious disruption of the current organisation of work in particular sectors, and a dispersal of centres of working-class power and organisation. The effect of technical change in the late eighteenth-century weaving industry, for example, was to increase employment in the industry, but at the same time breaking the organisation of the handloom weavers. A similar effect might occur in industries like printing today. Second, new technology is often designed to increase management control over work and reduce the possibility of workers determining their own pace of work and work practices. The word processor in the office, for example, allows regular monitoring of progress in a way that would not be possible with typists. Finally, there is scope for struggle over the distribution of the gains in productivity between wages and profits.

The trade union response to new technology has concentrated upon the protection of employment and a struggle over any income gains which may arise. The idea put forward by the TUC of 'New Technology Agreements' negotiated between trade unions and management to control the introduction of new technology is an important development. The TUC has issued a 'Checklist for Negotiators' for these agreements covering information disclosure, employment and output plans, retraining, hours of work and control over work and health and safety. Key elements in the trade union response have been the aims of deploying income gains in an expansion of public service employment. These aims need to be integrated within the AES.

## 5. Other Approaches To Reducing Unemployment

We have so far argued that the basis of a return to full employment should be a policy for expansion. There are a number of different approaches to reducing unemployment which have support within the Labour movement and which need to be considered— reduction in working hours, special employment and training measures, workers' plans and local authority enterprise. We see them as potentially important *defensive* responses in circumstances in which an AES is not possible, and important elements of a plan for employment *within* an AES. In isolation, however, (while they may be highly desirable in themselves) they would have little impact on the level of employment.

### Working Time

The campaign for a shorter working week has won widespread support in the trade union movement. It is not just seen as one response to unemployment generated by technological change. Struggles to reduce working time have a long history going back to the agitation over the ten hour day in the nineteenth century. Nevertheless the debates around the 35 hour week and the issue of new technology cannot be considered in isolation from one another.

Unquestionably the objective of reducing time spent at work and expanding leisure time must be part of any socialist programme. But what impact would a reduction in the working week have on unemployment? Attempts at quantifying the number of jobs which could be 'created' by negotiating shorter working time frequently do no more than express the mechanical consequences of redefining a full-time job to consist of 35 instead of 40 hours of labour time: they take no account of the actual economic relationships of a capitalist system of production and exchange. If working time is reduced with no loss of weekly earnings then hourly earnings obviously rise (assuming that a reduction in 'normal hours' is not just met with an increase in overtime). If output per worker each hour does not rise when working hours fall, then the company will have to take on more workers to produce the same level of output. However costs per unit of production will clearly rise and the company can cover this rise either by raising its prices by the same proportion or by taking a cut in profits. If prices are raised generally then the cut in working hours will have produced a drop in real earnings from those employed.

If on the other hand productivity does rise as working hours fall, then there is no reason to take on any extra workers because the size of the market will not have changed and all variables will remain unchanged except for hours worked. Thus there are a number of possible outcomes: no change in employment, or a possible rise in employment with either a fall in real wages or a fall in profit. We discuss the role of profit in Chapter 6 where we argue that although profit is not a crucial determinant of firms' decisions, persistently low profit without counteracting policies will adversely affect investment and employment.

So unless we are prepared to see a substantial fall in profit and take the consequences, 'work sharing' means wage sharing. It is interesting that there are two approaches to the demand for a shorter working week. On the one hand some make attempts to convince employers that there will be *benefits* from shorter working time. Others put forward the demand for an immediate 35 hour week with no loss of pay in the knowledge that it could not be conceded without major disruption. The latter approach perhaps draws on a clearer understanding of the consequences, but is based on a political strategy of 'exposing' capitalism by mobilising people around popular but non-realisable slogans, which we reject.

Thus demands for higher employment on the basis of a shorter working week often either accept the constraints on expansion and seek work-sharing at the expense of real wages (without the guarantee of more jobs), or are part of a strategy of deliberate disruption. We would argue for a much more positive approach which recognises that work-sharing under capitalism cannot be an answer to the short-term crisis of unemployment, but which sees reduced working time, and more flexibility in working hours as important ways of making sure that expansion under an AES has the maximum impact on employment. This is not to underestimate the political importance of demands over working time in defensive struggles by the trade union movement to counter the effects of the crisis and the re-structuring of industry along capitalist lines.

### Special Measures

A second response to unemployment is to propose employment subsidies, job creation schemes and training programmes such as those which proliferated under the Labour Government. The Labour movement has naturally welcomed these schemes and defended them against Tory attack—but we must be honest in recognising their limitations. First their function can be simply cosmetic—to cover up politically unacceptable jobless figures by temporarily removing some people from the dole queue. They can thus provide a substitute for a real programme to reduce unemployment and improve training, and can be used to fragment and manipulate the unemployed. Second the effect of schemes such as the Temporary Employment Subsidy (TES) (which has now been phased out) is uncertain. To the extent that employment in subsidised firms is actually boosted, rather than just their profits, it could be argued that the additional output simply creates unemployment in competing domestic firms, or that the taxes used to pay the subsidy are a drain on profits generally. In practice the TES was a disguised import control in industries such as textiles, which is why the EEC Commission insisted that it be phased out. Our point is that training schemes and the creation of socially useful jobs in the public sector must have a part to play in a programme to reduce unemployment, but the dangers and limitations of employment subsidies and training schemes must be recognised. They can never be a substitute for a full AES.

### Workers' Plans

The third response we discuss is the argument that the way to create jobs is by encouraging groups of workers to develop alternative plans of production, including production of socially useful products. Again, while such plans can be extremely valuable in organising opposition to redundancy it would be quite wrong to exaggerate their potential for employment creation and misleading to pose workers' plans as an alternative to an AES. Production only creates jobs if the products can be sold. Production for social use is nothing more than a romantic fantasy unless there is some way of transforming social needs into effective demand—in other words control over the allocation of public spending.

We return to this question in Chapter 7.

## *Local Authority Schemes*

The main centre for opposition to the course of the crisis is the trade union movement, but Labour-controlled local authorities can also play an important role. The London Labour Party has put forward a proposal for a local Enterprise Board under the Greater London Council which would provide finance and advice for setting up cooperatives and other ventures. This is an important initiative which could be taken up by local authorities in other areas.

## 6 Skill Shortages

A final difficulty which we raise is the problem of shortages of specific kinds of labour which may arise in a rapid expansion of production. The problem of skilled labour shortages, even at substantial levels of unemployment, is often used by the Right as an argument against reflating the economy. The problem however must be seen in perspective. A recent study by the Department of Employment concluded:

"Some alleged skill shortages disappear on closer investigation. It is not uncommon to find . . . that some are short-lived, and others are attributable to factors other than the availability of skilled labour . . . there may be discrepancies between allegations from external sources and the true needs of the company."

Moreover we should recognise the impact of the sharp drop of nearly 40% in the intake of apprentices in the engineering industry between 1970-71 and 1972-73. The previous level of apprenticeships has not yet been restored even with substantial government aid. Apprenticeships are thus one expense that private firms cut back on in the recession. Our view is that there may be short-term problems but these can be overcome by greater job security which will bring flexibility. In the medium term the answer will lie in an expansion of training and a transformation of the labour process to give the skilled worker greater control.

## 7. Conclusion

In this chapter we have made the case that the jobs crisis can only be tackled through a comprehensive AES and that the goal of full employment is a central, and realisable, objective of that strategy. We have argued that a programme of expansion at a realistic rate coupled with reductions in working hours and special employment measures could succeed in bringing about a rapid fall in unemployment.

The demand for full employment is based not only on a concern for social welfare. It is a challenge to the idea that people's lives should be determined by blind market forces and the pursuit of profit by finance and big business. Moreover it is an assertion of strength by the Labour movement against those who seek to weaken it. It is worth remembering that the Depression of the thirties was brought to an end only by war. The challenge we face in the eighties is to restore full employment through a socialist economic strategy.

# The Industrial Strategy

## 1. Introduction

A programme for the regeneration of industry under democratic control must lie at the heart of the Alternative Economic Strategy. There are four kinds of problems such a programme would have to deal with. The first is to ensure that production responds to an expansion of demand. We argued in general terms in Chapter 4 that management of aggregate demand was inadequate without intervention on the supply side. In the circumstances in which an AES would come to be implemented this general problem would be exacerbated by the fact that sections of industry will have been run down and will have adjusted to lower levels of production by eliminating spare capacity. It may also be exacerbated by a political response from industry. The implementation of an AES would be an assertion of political strength by the Labour movement. Business would naturally recognise this and express their fears, in typical indirect forms such as a drop in 'business confidence', or warnings of higher inflation and reduced investment.

But in addition to these short-term 'conjunctural' problems, an industrial strategy would have to deal with the long-term structural decline of industry. It would have to check and reverse the process of 'deindustrialisation'. An approach to dealing with this problem, based on detailed planning, selective public ownership, and control of finance for investment, has been discussed in the Labour movement for some time but is now coming to be seen as part of an integrated economic strategy.

Thirdly, an industrial strategy should seek to control the long-term forms of development of industry—planning its regional distribution, taking a view as to the kind of industrial structure we would wish to promote, particularly as oil production declines in the 1990s, intervening actively to create new industries where they do not at present exist and guiding the development and introduction of new technology.

Finally, central to the strategy must be moves towards real, and not just token, democracy in industry, involving workers at all levels from the shopfloor (and office floor) upwards. This is crucial because any industrial strategy which pursued efficiency at the expense of trade union control of the production process, which pursued rationalisation in opposition to the workers involved, or which sought to increase investment merely by subsidising pre-existing management plans, could not claim to be a socialist strategy, and would not generate widespread support within the organised working class, without which it would not succeed.

In this chapter we discuss some of the proposals for industrial strategy which have been developed in the Labour movement and assess their claims to be able to deal with the first three problems outlined above. The question of workers' control and industrial democracy is taken up in more detail in Chapter 7. We begin by briefly reviewing the evidence of deindustrialisation and trying to put the problem of manufacturing industry in a broader perspective of economic planning. We then outline the industrial strategy commonly associated with the AES and contrast it with the 'industrial strategy' pursued by the last Labour Government. The three areas of the strategy – planning, public ownership and control of finance – are discussed in more detail.

Our broad conclusion is that the proposals for planning agreements. a planning commission, selective public ownership through a reformed National Enterprise Board, and measures to control the allocation and use of finance, represent the basis of a potentially viable and progressive industrial strategy. However there is an urgent need to think through the way these proposals fit together, the practical details of implementation and the tactics of overcoming the opposition from business which is inevitable. Moreover, it is vital to take the debate beyond the case for replacing private capitalist control, to develop an understanding of the purpose and criteria for democratic social control of industry.

## 2. The Decline Of Industry

In Chapter 2 we gave an account of the economic crisis, arguing that the policies of the present Government were exacerbating a long-term structural weakness of industry in Britain. It is useful to summarise the main features of this process of deindustrialisation.

* The output of manufacturing industry reached a peak in 1973 which it has not since regained. At present output is falling sharply and is currently not far above the level reached in 1968.

* Employment in manufacturing has fallen by 1½ million since 1970. As a percentage of the total labour force it has declined from 39% to 31%.
* Productivity in manufacturing industry has grown far more slowly than in most industrialised countries as the following figures suggest:

*Table 6.1*

| | Change in output per worker in manufacturing between 1965 and 1973 | Investment per Employee in Manufacturing 1970-74 £1 |
| --- | --- | --- |
| Japan | +112% | 530 |
| Netherlands | + 77% | 580 |
| West Germany | + 54% | 450 |
| Italy | + 50% | 320 |
| France | + 48% | 540 |
| UK | + 33% | 240 |
| US | + 31% | 740 |

1. 1970 prices; average annual rate of investment over the period.

* Along with this poor productivity growth, the UK has been the only major country in which employment and output in manufacturing have declined in absolute terms and as a proportion of total output.
* The failure of investment in Britain is well known. The figures in Table 6.1 show how between 1970 and 1974 investment per worker in British manufacturing was less than half that in Japan or France and less than a third of the level in the United States.
* The consequence of persistent underinvestment is that workers in this country are forced to work with out-of-date equipment and less capital. One estimate is that the fixed assets per worker in manufacturing in the UK amounted to £7,500 as compared with £23 000 in West Germany and £30,000 in Japan (F. E. Jones; *National Westminster Bank Review*, May 1978).

The consequences of this decline have been insecurity of employment, poor working conditions and persistent attempts by management to improve competitiveness by forcing down wages and undermining trade union control at the point of production. We made some attempt to account for the process of decline in Chapter 3, drawing attention to the degree of concentration of industry and the dominant position of companies with international interests, the way in which the relations between industry and the financial system have stifled growth, the influence of the City in the formation of economic policy, the defensive strength of the trade union movement in production and the declining level of profitability.

It does not help to look for simple processes of cause and effect: low investment is as much a consequence of industrial decline as a cause, while low profitability is as much a symptom of inadequate investment as a determinant. We are faced with processes of circular and cumulative causation which will continue as long as financial Capital has the freedom to move in search of the cheapest labour and highest return, as long as multinational companies have the autonomy to determine where and when to site their production without regard for the social consequences of their decisions, and as long as private profitability determined on the international market is taken as the arbiter of social need and useful production.

If the past looks bad, the future appears disastrous. From the Government's own forecasts manufacturing output is expected to be over 6% lower in 1984 than when it took office. There are few who would regard this as anything other than highly optimistic. The monetarist assault on industry, combining high interest rates, falling demand, an overvalued pound, restrictions on the availability of credit and cuts in aid to industry, is designed to precipitate a radical and traumatic restructuring of industry and of relations between Capital and Labour — a crisis in the classic sense.

It may be argued that this could lay the basis for a period of renewed growth along capitalist lines but we would suggest a more likely outcome is accelerated industrial decline, growing overseas penetration of domestic markets and a further shift in both UK and foreign-based multi-nationals away from production in the UK. The immense costs being stored for the future will only be partly and temporarily disguised by the contribution of North Sea oil to government revenues and to the Balance of Payments. Talk of wholesale destruction of key manufacturing sectors is not entirely far fetched — the prospect over the next few years of the economy losing virtually all of the textile, clothing and footwear industries, and a sufficient proportion of the steel and motor vehicle industries seriously to hinder future expansion, is not unreal.

Before moving on to look at the way the AES responds to this industrial crisis it is worth looking at the argument, recently advanced by John Kay and Peter Forsyth and eagerly taken up by Tory spokesmen, that the decline of manufacturing industry is an inevitable consequence of North Sea oil production. They purport to show that the only way that the fruits of the North Sea can be transformed into goods and services which contribute to welfare, is by accepting the increased importation of manufactured goods which would partly displace home production.
home manufacturing production.

That such a proposition can be treated as a serious contribution is a measure of the depths to which economic debate in this country has sunk. Of course oil production has consequences for the manufacturing sector, but it is ridiculous to suggest that the consequences should necessarily be an overvalued pound rather than a relaxation of the Balance of Payments constraint, an absolute decline of manufacturing output rather than a smaller share of growing total output, and the import of consumer goods rather than increased investment in domestic manufacturing. The challenge is to ensure that the temporary benefits provided by North Sea oil are invested at home to ensure collective prosperity when those resources are exhausted.

## 3. The Industrial Strategy

We would argue that the industrial decline described above cannot be dealt with without a radical new approach to industry based on planning, public ownership, control of finance and moves towards workers' control, aimed at reducing the autonomy of Capital.

The basic elements of the industrial strategy developed in the Labour movement are reasonably well known, although there are many different interpretations and differences of emphasis. First there should be planning agreements negotiated between individual 'Category I' companies (the top 100 or so companies), the government and the relevant trade unions. These agreements would be obligatory and would be backed by sanctions, such as making the availability of public finance and tax relief dependent on an agreement being reached. Second, public ownership would be extended to key firms in each sector of manufacturing industry by the National Enterprise Board (NEB) and other state holding companies, using powers of compulsory acquisition. Such firms would then act as leaders in those sectors, through expanded investment, acting as an example to guide the level of investment of other firms in the sector. Third, it would be necessary to co-ordinate the planning activities at the level of the firm and sector with policies determining behaviour at an aggregate level, through some form of National Planning Commission. Fourth, some control of the financial system, through public ownership and channelling of institutional funds, would be necessary to ensure that the financial resources necessary for a substantial increase in industrial investment would be made available.

This brief sketch sums up the main points which can be found elaborated in *'Labour's Programme'*, in statements such as *'Labour and Industry'* (1975), and in numerous TUC and Labour Party Conference resolutions. It will be immediately obvious that there are many important questions which need to be asked before we can judge the worth of such a strategy. But first let us establish how little this approach has in common with that actually taken by the Labour government in the 74-79 period. The superficial correspondences stand as a warning to anyone who imagines that legislation or institutional reform alone are sufficient to constitute a strategy.

The Industry Act passed at the end of 1975, which set up the NEB and provided a statutory framework for planning agreements, was the outcome of a series of political defeats for the Left – such as the removal of Eric Heffer and then Tony Benn from the Department of Industry and the loss from the Bill of crucial powers. It followed the defeat in the EEC referendum in June and the acceptance by the trade union movement of the £6 limit on pay rises.

If we look at the provisions of the Act we see that most remain unused – such as those for the disclosure of information – while only two planning agreements were actually concluded. The first with Chrysler proved to be a sick joke when only two years later the company was taken over by Peugeot, after being allocated £162.5m of public money. The second was with the National Coal Board – again a parody of the original intentions behind the proposals. The NEB took on a role as a convenient insulator for the government from the difficult problems of rescued firms such as BL, Rolls Royce and Alfred Herbert. In addition it has acted as a merchant bank to a number of small companies. The only major initiative it has taken has been in the field of micro-electronics.

So the 1975 Act was not important to the government's 'industrial strategy' which was launched at a meeting of the National Economic Development Committee in November 1975. Rather the strategy was based on tripartite discussions in a series of about 40 'sector working parties' (SWPs) covering selected sectors or subsectors of manufacturing industry. This structure was tied in with a number of schemes to subsidise investment operated under the Conservatives' own Industry Act passed in 1972, and a set of macro-economic policies and tax incentives designed to boost industrial profits—such as tax relief on stock appreciation. Interestingly enough some of the most direct intervention was carried out separately, and with virtually no accountability, by the Bank of England—for example in the bread and clothing industries. But generally the rhetoric of industrial strategy provided a cover for both a fairly traditional set of macro-economic policies designed to appease 'business confidence', and for a variety of ad hoc interventions.

The Government industrial strategy was inspired and co-ordinated by the National Economic Development Office, the 'planning' body set up by the Conservatives in 1962. It was significant in that it marked a recognition of the need for a 'supply side' policy as a counterpart to the abandonment of demand management. By concentrating on the sectoral level, the strategy sought to build up a consensus between management and labour away from the political conflict at the level of the individual company and the shop floor, and at the level of Parliament. Since the working parties were based on bringing together the main competing firms, the basis for co-operation was collective action to reduce import penetration and increase exports, and joint competition for government funds against other sectors. As a strategy for raising competitiveness it was probably more developed than the Left's industrial strategy which it was brought in to replace.

There are a number of important lessons to be drawn from this experience for the implementation of an AES. First there was blanket opposition to the Left's approach from the civil service and the CBI. This must be expected, and although civil service opposition can be undermined by changes in the appointment system, by strengthening of the role of political advisors and taking other such measures, the CBI can only be hostile. The key problem in 1974/5 was that there was so little understanding of and support for the Left's industrial strategy in the Labour movement that it could be ditched without serious opposition. Second, little attempt appears to have been made to involve the trade union movement in the formulation or implementation of the Benn-Heffer approach. The TUC has never taken the idea of planning agreements seriously, and threw its full weight behind the tripartite strategy launched in 1975. The commitment of trade unionists, if not of trade union leaderships, is a precondition of success.

Finally, it could be argued that the formulation of the Benn-Heffer industrial strategy was seriously deficient, lacking both theoretical and analytical underpinning and a clear conception of its implementation. In particular no attempt was made to link it with policies of demand management or planning of trade. These criticisms do not signal our rejection of the thinking behind the strategy, which we broadly support, but rather the urgent need to develop a much clearer idea of the aims, institutions and instruments of industrial strategy and the ways in which it must be integrated into a comprehensive AES.

## 4. Objectives Of Planning

The Tories have adopted a radical strategy of strengthening market forces at the expense of intervention at the level of firm or sector, and any alternative to monetarism must entail a reversal of this process and a move towards greater social control over production: in other words some form of planning in a weak or strong sense. Yet there has been very little serious debate about economic planning. One source of confusion is that 'planning' can mean:

* *formulating intentions* for action (for example, when the government sets its public expenditure plans):
* *setting targets* for broad macro-economic aggregates (as in the National Plan of 1965);
* attempting to influence private sector behaviour by '*indication*' or fixing market signals (e.g. farm price policy);
  **or**
* determining private sector behaviour by *direction*.

One consequence of this confusion is that Left and Right can happily agree on the need for 'planning' with entirely different processes in mind. We will try and make clear which of these senses of the word we are using. We will begin by discussing the objectives of planning and then go on to look at the instruments and institutions proposed.

The simple account of the objectives of planning often given on the Left is that the problem with the economy is its lack of competitiveness and poor trade performance; this is caused by a weak manufacturing sector, the result of underinvestment and poor management; and an important cause of underinvestment is seen as lack of finance. The solution which naturally follows is to increase the supply of investment finance and plan to achieve some target—say a doubling in five years—for investment in the manufacturing sector. Protection may be justified while this is being done but would be removed once competitiveness is restored. We think that each of the steps in this very common argument needs to be looked at very closely.

First: is the attention paid to manufacturing industry justified? After all, manufacturing provides less than a third of total output in the economy and, rather surprisingly, its productivity (output per worker) is lower than other sectors of the economy, and has been so at least since 1945.

One answer which may be given is this: "Obviously manufacturing industry produces the real wealth of the economy, the real things which support the public sector and the service sector." Underlying this response there is often a view, which we suspect is common in the Labour movement, that manufacturing is in some sense 'productive' while other sectors are not.

We see this as a very dangerous position because it gives rise to quite false views about the relations between public and private sectors and can be used to justify cuts in public spending to transfer resources to the 'wealth-creating' sector away from the 'wealth-consuming' sector. This was an argument which appeared to convince the industrial unions of the need for cuts in 1976. For example, the TUC-Labour Party Liaison Committee statement published in that year stated:

> " We must give far greater emphasis to the needs of manu-
> facturing industry. That is why the government has decided to
> level off public spending from April 1977 onwards."

It is certainly a valuable propaganda weapon in the current Tory attack on the public sector. We should be quite clear, first, that the public sector is just as productive of wealth—real useful goods and services like buildings, health and education—as the manufacturing sector. Secondly we should be clear that cuts in public spending do nothing whatsoever to transfer resources into manufacturing industry. They merely help to cut demand for industry's products, which induces a slow-down in investment and a cut in employment.

Thus we must be very careful to avoid using the claims of industry as a cover for an attack on the public sector. Having said that, we should recognise that the real importance of manufacturing industry is not that it is more 'productive' but, first, that it is crucial for international trade and second, that it provides somewhat greater scope for increases in productivity. Manufacturing industry will not provide a significant increase in employment, but it is essential to halt its decline in order to ensure that the country can sustain a level of exports necessary to pay for the level of imports which can be anticipated at full employment with associated trade controls. Thus we support the view that a strategy for manufacturing industry is central but argue that it is important to reject claims that it has higher status as a 'wealth-creating' sector, or that cuts in public spending are necessary to expand the manufacturing sector.

Turning to the question of investment, we should be wary of assuming either that low investment is the main cause of decline or that higher levels of investment necessarily provide a solution. We argued above that the low level of investment in manufacturing on international comparisons was in many ways a *symptom* of decline. While higher investment would almost certainly be welcome as part of a broader industrial strategy we should be careful not to dissassociate the question of 'how much' investment from questions of 'where', 'in what', 'when' and most importantly 'under whose control and with what consequences for the Labour process'. New technology for example is not a neutral advance, but is almost always associated with moves to increase management control over production as in the case of word processors, electronic newsgathering, computer typesetting or robots on the production line. For Capital the aim is clear: to increase efficiency and control. For Labour the options are less clear cut. Is it enough simply to defend traditional technologies and work practices and ignore the consequences for efficiency?

The third stage in the argument which needs to be questioned is that the objective of planning in the long term is to allow the economy to adjust without too much disruption to the pattern of production determined by world market forces; in other words to restore international competitiveness by means other than wage cuts. We argue at some length in Chapter 9 our general view that the market is an instrument of social control—of class rule—and on this basis we would suggest that when combined with the planning of trade, the objectives of industrial planning should not necessarily be tied to market criteria of what should or should not be produced.

Finally, the argument that the way to increase investment is to 'channel finance' is taken up in more detail below. To conclude this discussion of the objectives of planning, we suggest some themes which might be developed in future work. The basic question is: how do we go beyond the criteria of private profitability while retaining some kind of social efficiency in the allocation of resources? One answer is to develop a 'social audit' approach to project appraisal within the enterprise which takes into account the long-term social costs and benefits of the options available. This approach has to be made fairly systematic (including employment, regional and other criteria) in order to allow sensible allocation of finance on 'non-commercial' terms, rather than arbitrary and ad hoc financing in response to purely political pressures. At a broader level we need some framework for pushing the industrial structure towards or away from high technology sectors. The present approach seems to be to see what the Americans and Japanese are getting into, and see if we can chase them without being left behind. Finally, to present a convincing case for planning capable of winning propular support we must be able to back up our general proposals with specific and detailed recommendations for particular sectors, with thorough analysis of developments in each sector identifying the key firms involved.

Thus, to supplant the operation of the market it is essential that substitute mechanisms are developed which can effectively — and in a non-authoritarian manner — solve the problem of meeting consumer needs, efficiently allocate social labour and motivate those who perform labour.

## 5. Instruments Of Planning

The central instrument of planning envisaged in the industrial strategy would be the planning agreement — an agreement negotiated annually, but for a five-year period — which would cover the main strategic decisions taken by companies on investment levels and location, employment, price policy and the like. It would be negotiated between management and government with the trade unions playing an important role. The government would have available a variety of sanctions and incentives to enforce agreement including allocation of selective aid  discretionary tax relief, control of funds channelled through a National Investment Bank and Investment Reserve Fund, public purchasing policy, planning permission and permission for price increases. These could in theory be used equally against opposition to the government's plans from management or unions. A final sanction of nationalisation in cases of obstinate non-co-operation would also be available.

In addition, some proponents of Labour's industrial strategy have argued that the behaviour of private sector firms could be moulded by competition from the publicly-owned firms, controlled by the

NEB. We have reservations about this approach, particularly if it assumes that industry's problem is lack of competition, as in most sectors this is clearly not the case. However there may be some scope for the action of publicly-owned firms reinforcing, for example in their investment strategies, the pressures imposed on private firms through planning agreements. We should not however underestimate the problems. The workers in a company faced with bankruptcy because of competition from a public firm receiving subsidies or operating with lower rates of return will be just as vocal as its owners in opposing 'unfair' competition from the state. This of course is why one of the cardinal principles of the present structure of aid is 'non-discrimination' between competing domestic companies. Where selective aid is granted it is usually justified in terms of providing regional employment or favouring domestic against overseas industry.

The concept of planning agreements has great strengths. In particular it seeks to intervene where decisions are actually made, and seeks detailed control over the large companies which determine the economy. It has strengths also in that it can be seen as recognising that the problem of planning is not simply a technical problem of co-ordination, of supervising the allocation of resources. Industry will continue to be based on conflict — on class struggle — and so we would see planning as growing out of one basic expression of that conflict — collective bargaining. We would envisage the extension of collective bargaining to cover issues beyond wages and conditions — investment strategies, employment policies, etc. — taking the form of planning agreements with government representation. This would be one way of ensuring democracy in the planning process and avoiding the danger of its degenerating into simple corporatism. It does raise problems however where collective bargaining is absent or is not conducted at the level of the enterprise.

But having emphasised those strengths we need to recognise points of weakness which need to be developed. First the concentration on the level of the firm has distracted attention from the problem of linking planning at different levels of the economy, of integrating planning at the sectoral and national level. The objectives set through planning agreements could be co-ordinated with the work being done by the Sector Working Parties and with the wider plans for expansion of the economy, through a national planning agency. The techniques of input-output planning which make explicit the sectoral implications of macro-economic objectives could be used. But to follow through this co-ordinated approach, an agency with higher status and with more resources than has so far been envisaged would be necessary.

Second, a major barrier which arises when planning moves from the sectoral to the firm level is that serious discussion of plans requires disclosure of precisely that strategic information which any competing oligopolist cannot afford to disclose. As long as commercial secrecy is respected then it is difficult to see how the process can be democratic. If it is abandoned then the opposition will certainly be more serious and the state is necessarily going to be much more closely involved in arbitrating the market share of competing capitalists.

Third, it is not entirely clear what role profit is supposed to play in the whole process. One clear effect of industrial decline is a low rate of return on capital which industry will always argue is the obstacle to higher investment. Can this obstacle be surmounted through planning, or will the objective of planning be higher rates of profit? We would argue that the level of profit need not be the determining factor as long as appropriate accompanying policies are adopted. Profit performs three distinct roles: providing finance for investment, providing incentive to the owners of capital to invest, and more generally acting as a signal through which the market allocates capital resources. Each of these roles can be to some extent supplanted: the first by providing external finance, the second by using appropriate sanctions and non-profit incentives and the third by adopting a system of planned non-market or social criteria for the allocation of finance. These steps must be taken within an AES.

The final difficulty with the strategy of planning agreements is perhaps the most fundamental. It can be argued that as long as Capital remains in private hands it will do all it can to subvert attempts at planning and to resist the imposition of social control. Capitalist opposition to a thorough policy of planning could certainly be anticipated. Moreover it is not difficult to see that any measures taken to deal with this problem through the exercise of more direct control by the government or the trade unions would simply harden the opposition of Capital and could result in an all-out investment strike. Traditionally it is in the financial sphere that the economic effects of these political conflicts are most obvious—capitalists refuse to buy government debt and shift their capital overseas.

Whether this opposition could be overcome is a matter of judgement. We believe that it could, provided the rationale for planning was broadly understood and supported and provided the workforce of the companies involved were committed to its implementation.

## 6. Selective Public Ownership

Public ownership is a crucial part of the AES. However, widespread nationalisation is simply not popular. Of course the role of the media and business anti-nationalisation campaigns must be taken into account, but it is important to look for deeper reasons for working-class opposition. The fact is that the experience of nationalisation, however much we may condemn the failure to 'socialise' the public sector, has not been such as to give support for a socialist case for public ownership. The way that nationalised companies have in practice operated, particularly in so far as the socialist criteria of production for social need and democratic forms of management are concerned, has not differed greatly from firms in the private sector. Nationalisation is in no sense a panacea – rather it is the beginning of the real problem. It is the point at which the Labour movement is forced to find answers to the question of what are the *socialist* criteria for organising production and managing enterprises which can replace the all-pervasive 'logic' of capitalism. The failure to confront this problem seriously may be counted as an important reason why there is so little popular support for a programme of widespread nationalisation in this country. Public ownership is identified, however unjustified this may be, with inefficiency and bureaucracy.

This is where the AES, with its industrial strategy combining a progressive extension of public ownership of dominant profitable firms and overall planning – by direct and indirect means – of the remaining private firms is at its strongest and yet at its most vulnerable. It provides the opportunity for new forms of successful public ownership, allowing new relationships between worforce and management – and provides hope for improvement in areas where there is a popular perception of failure. Yet by moving selectively into markets which are competitive both domestically and internationally, the strategy subjects the new public enterprises to the logic of capitalism even more directly than the existing public monopolies. It will require a political determination so far not much in evidence from those who will be presumably relied on to carry out these policies to ensure that the new criteria are developed and rigorously applied.

This immediately raises questions about the provision of finance for investment and the terms of its provision, the attitudes towards pay and redundancies of the new democratic controllers, and the forms of democracy within the public enterprise sector. It must be accepted that industrial restructuring, for example to accomodate the exports of manufactured goods from some developing countries, will involve the closure of some plants. The ability to deal with this problem, by ensuring full consultation with the trade unions, involvement of the workforce in the consideration of alternatives, redeployment and retraining of displaced labour etc., will be one of the key tests of the strategy. It must be emphasised though that these problems cannot be treated in isolation from the rest of the economy—in conditions of full employment decisions about restructuring are very different from those taken when every job must be defended.

It is obvious that a radical reappraisal of the role of the NEB would be necessary were it to move from its present roles to become an agency of progressive public enterprise as outlined above. To ask for more money to finance its activities is simply not enough. Clearly its powers of acquisition would have to be strengthened, its guidelines rewritten, its operations made more democratic and its management changed. The Left of the Labour Party is sometimes too easily taken in by superficial similarities of form which disguise fundamental differences in content and practice.

## 7. Control And Allocation Of Finance

An important theme in current Labour movement proposals on industrial strategy is that finance should be made available for investment through public channels. In particular, the money collected in the form of long-term savings by the Pension Funds and Life Assurance Companies (over £9,000 million in 1979) and the huge revenues expected from North Sea oil production (estimated to rise to as much as £24,000 million a year at current prices by 1985) should be channelled into investment in industry. The mechanism now proposed to ensure that this takes place is a National Investment Bank taking 10% of the new money from the institutions (on which it would give a guaranteed return) and an equal amount contributed by the government. The TUC has proposed that the Bank should have a tripartite management board and would make available money, at non-commercial rates where necessary, for projects identified through sector working parties or, presumably, through planning agreements.

It would be extremely important to link such a bank into the overall planning system. To invest successfully sums of up to £2,000 million a year—when we remember that the *total* fixed investment by manufacturing industry last year was only £6,500 million—is a major undertaking. Previous private bodies set up to channel institutional money such as Finance for Industry (FFI) have not succeeded in finding investments even for the tiny funds at their disposal. Agreeing investment decisions through planning agreements could be an important way of identifying suitable projects and the allocation of finance could in turn be a valuable way of reinforcing those agreements.

Finally it is worth mentioning briefly the other projects which the Labour Party has adopted as its official policy. First there is public ownership of the four main clearing Banks and top seven insurance companies, which could allow a greater control over the allocation of credit. Second there is a proposal for an Investment Reserve Fund through which a proportion of pre-tax profits would be placed in 'blocked balances' and released either for specific investments or at specific times. Finally there are proposals for reform of the Bank of England and the creation of a State Bank from a merger of the National Savings Bank and Girobank. It is important that these various proposals are brought together in a way which ensures that financial control gives support to industrial planning.

To sum up, we have outlined and tried to provide some justification for the industrial strategy advanced within the AES, while at the same time recognising some of its weaknesses and raising some questions which we feel need to be debated much more thoroughly. In particular we need to discuss the objectives of social control of industry and the criteria for operation of firms under workers' or public control.

# Workers' Control and Local Struggles

## 1. Introduction

The AES seeks to achieve a resolution of the current crisis in a manner which leaves the working class in a stronger position and exposes further contradictions in our system of political economy.

Attainment of these objectives will require the mobilisation of considerable political support among the working class in all its organisational forms, among working people as individuals, and among broadly-based interest groups of various kinds. There is little prospect of the successful implementation of the AES unless this mobilisation occurs. For a socialist government to come to power and implement a set of policies entailing such a radical break from orthodox political economy will only be possible on the basis of a significant change in the distribution of power in our society.

The implication of this requirement is that the AES must become more than a set of policy demands — however coherent and justified. The development of the AES must be firmly rooted in working-class and popular concerns. For this to occur there are two essential prerequisites:

1 The policy demands themselves must arise out of the everyday experience and needs of the working class in their working, social and home lives.
2 The policy demands must not be regarded simply as a 'manifesto' for the next Labour Government, but must become the object of the current campaigning and direct action by all working-class organisations and by broadly-based interest groups.

It follows from this that it will be necessary to examine how the various forms of struggle and means of organisational expression could be used to advance the AES. It is important to reiterate that while some formulations of the AES appear to regard it as something fixed or static in composition, in fact we cannot define the AES precisely — nor would we wish to do so, for fear of hindering its development. Even at the most simple level, the forms of action will themselves modify and develop the initial demands.

## 2. The State And The Issue Of 'Freedom'

There is another sense in which the adoption and development of the AES by the Labour movement raises fundamental issues. The role of the state and the methods and objectives of state intervention are central to the socialist concept of the AES. Objections from the Right that state intervention implies a deprivation of freedom and the installation of authoritarian forms of political control are matched by objections from the Left that the AES represents a new move towards a corporate state and that, in any event, while capitalist society remains, the state and its interventions will remain indelibly capitalist and thus inimical to working-class interests. While we have strong objections to both of these views of the nature of the AES, they do emphasise a key problem faced by its proponents.

How in precise terms can the intervention and activities of the state during the transition to socialism be made democratic and freedom-enhancing? Part of the answer lies in the 'organic' form of the AES: it is not a completed blueprint, but an indicative programme. The remainder of the answer lies in firmly linking the AES to the development of workers' control and to corresponding attempts at increasing autonomy in other areas of political life. No one on the Left should be deceived by philosophically naive arguments about individual freedom which imply that freedom is somehow the property of, or an attribute of, the individual. Freedom arises in collective action, out of the interactions and sometimes the conflicts between people engaged in social activity—particularly production. Provided the modifications of the present system of political economy amplify and extend collective influence over the social activities of production, distribution and consumption then freedom—socialist freedom—will be enlarged, not reduced.

How then shall the AES be organically linked to the development of workers' control and other autonomous movements—movements as varied as residents' associations, local consumer groups, Anti-Nazi League activities, or anti-nuclear campaigns, all of which attempt to challenge bureaucratic forms of control and generate independent political positions? To answer this question, even in outline, is difficult. It will be necessary first to examine the current debate on workers control, and then the development of issue politics outside the workplace.

## 3. Workers' Control

The movement for workers' control has a long history in the UK and in Continental Europe, particularly France and Italy. It stems from the syndicalist movement in the 19th century, but over the last decade or so, principally through the medium of the Institute for Workers' Control, the demand for an increased degree of workers' control has gained momentum. It has also been the case, particularly in the UK, that the strength of the British trade union movement at the point of production, and the attempts by management and employers to regain control of production in increasingly competitive market conditions, have led to debate and some experimentation in the field of 'industrial democracy'.

Pressures from below became more intense during the seventies. Occupations of factories in the UK and France and Italy (in France the occupation has long been a trade union weapon), the formation of workers' co-operatives and the publication of alternative plans of production, all took place as a response to closures and increasing unemployment.

In 1978 the Bullock Committee reported on the possibility of a legislative approach to the introduction of 'industrial democracy' via trade union representation at company board level. During the seventies both the TUC and the CBI formulated policies towards industrial democracy and individual unions took up various and conflicting positions on the subject. The Labour Party also felt the need to enter the debate and produced its own suggested approach. In the event the Labour Government, itself split over what should be done, failed to implement either the Bullock Committee recommendations or any of its own.

How has the trade union movement in particular responded to the growing pressures for workers' control, and the contradictions which this raises in capitalist society? It is possible to identify conflicts and problems arising within trade union organisation as a result, for example, of the UCS struggle in the early seventies, the Lucas Aerospace Combine Committee's alternative plan and the Wales TUC's attempt to fight steel and coal closures by means of the general, political strike weapon. It is not clear that the full implications of these events have been appreciated in any depth by the trade union movement. As discussion of the Bullock Committee Report illustrated, the divisions in the trade union movement are considerable. There are those (e.g. the EEPTU) on the Right of the movement who argue that trade unions should not become involved in management, but should follow the US trade unions' tradition of simply bargaining over pay and conditions and leaving management to manage. This view has a strong echo on the Left with some unions (e.g. pre-Duffy AUEW) arguing that industrial democracy implies 'class collaboration' and is thus to be shunned. Then there are those unions (e.g. the GMWU) who argue against any rigid institutionalised form of employee participation and in favour of an extension of collective bargaining. Finally, the TGWU tends to campaign (though not strongly) in favour of some institutionalised form of industrial democracy along the lines of Bullock.

What approach, therefore, does the AES adopt towards the issue of workers' control? How much importance should be attached to it within the AES and what are the specific problems which it raises?

It must be stated immediately that within the AES we attach an overriding importance to the extension of workers' power—both at the point of production and within the wider democratic process of arriving at economic and social goals. The autonomous exercise of power by the working class is, in this sense, crucial to the achievement of democratic socialism and to its subsequent survival and growth.

This emphasis on workers' control has several different aspects. First it rests upon historical experience. It incorporates our awareness of the dangers attaching to bureaucratic forms of state power. It shows that we have learned the lessons of the Prague spring in 1968, and of the Lenin Shipyard in 1980.

Secondly, it links our strategy firmly to the existing institutions for the defence of working people, in particular the trade unions. The AES aims to build upon the actual strengths of the trade union movement, at the same time drawing it to new support and new popularity.

Thirdly, workers' control lies at the heart of our concept of socialism itself—or more precisely, our ideas about the *life* of socialist society. We have already argued that socialism will not be achieved solely by the enactment of legislation; while the role of state power in the AES is crucial, so is the power of working class and popular support. But even more importantly, the idea of democratic socialism, understood as a way of organising society on a continuing basis, is incoherent unless it is linked to the widest possible self-management by working people of their own lives. Social liberation, both in its attainment and in its future growth, cannot be contemplated except on the basis of the autonomous activity of working people. We must therefore begin the transition to socialism as we mean to go on.

The extension of workers' control, however, does raise specific organisational tasks. How would we seek to transform 'participative' structures existing in some sectors of work? What are the implications for the internal organisation of trade unions? We seek to answer these questions below.

Firstly, it must be recognised that at the moment there is little evidence of *genuine* worker participation in the planning of corporate strategy—even in the publicly owned sector. Where participation schemes exist, their normal purpose is to secure the commitment of workers or their trade unions to a corporate strategy devised essentially by management alone, and often involving significant loss of job control or security.

But clearly there would be dangers in a strategy which limited itself to enhancing the role of collective bargaining in the corporate planning process. These are the dangers of 'enterprise syndicalism'. The end result may simply be to strengthen capitalism by attaching workers more closely to the already existing enterprise objectives— that is, essentially, to the search for profitability in the context of capitalist markets. The danger of a movement towards workers' control degenerating in this way is also highlighted by the advocacy of a form of 'market socialism' by Peter Jay and David Owen. In their formulation, an attempt is made to secure the co-existence of industrial democracy and a 'mixed'—that is, predominantly capitalist—economy. Workers would be given formal control over their workplace, but would be subject to the 'discipline' of the market.

This consideration leads us to emphasise two distinctive features of the AES. Firstly, as we have argued, we attach a fundamental importance to the extension of organised working class power. But secondly, we place this development firmly in the context of a *planned* economy. This means that we seek to challenge not only the forms of control exercised directly in the workplace, but also the invisible coercion of the capitalist market. Changes in system objectives, away from production for profit towards production for social need, will be necessary genuinely to transform the types of decision made at enterprise level. The linkage in the AES between workers' control and the negotiation of planning agreements becomes self-evident. We see the planning process—described more fully in Chapter 6—as the essential environment in which the evolution of genuine workers' control might take place.

Secondly, what changes in trade union structure are implied by the move towards workers' control? The problems to be resolved and the choices to be made are not easy. The 'official' trade union movement may find difficulty in accepting powerful local shop steward involvement in corporate decision-making which may exclude full-time district officials, and cut across existing procedures. On the other hand to concede control of union policy at enterprise level to shop-stewards who may be unaware of, or prepared to ignore, wider considerations would be a danger not only to trade union control, but possibly to socialist advance.

Our view is that whatever the difficulties it is a necessary condition for the advance of democratic socialism that workers should have a say over decisions made at the point of production. But the clear implication for trade union structure is that local and regional activity and power must increase, with a greater role for branches, particularly workplace branches, in the formulation and implementation of union policy. Trades councils, for example, almost destroyed by the TUC in the 1950s, should regain the power which they once had.

## 4. Workers' Plans

There can be little doubt about the powerful influence that the development of the Lucas shop stewards' Alternative Corporate Plan has had on the UK Labour movements, and elsewhere in Europe. Other stewards have been encouraged to follow the example and there is evidence of the development of more thoughtful challenges to management control based on capitalist criteria. Such challenges, based on alternative economic premises which stress social objectives, are a useful practical teaching device to illustrate the contradictory and amoral nature of capitalism in operation. Nonetheless, it would be foolish to pretend that these plans can be presented as *solutions* to the problems of job loss and product choice within the framework of a capitalist economy. Indeed one aim of both the Lucas campaign and of the AES must surely be to demonstrate the limits of such an approach in an economy which is ultimately governed by the demands of private profit mediated through the forces of the market.

The most publicised aspect of such plans is the proposal for 'socially useful' production—i.e. alternative products to those for which there is no longer a market. The problem is that if such products are intended for sale to the public sector (like kidney machines) then the argument is really about the level and allocation of public spending If the products are intended for private markets or governments overseas and they can be sold at a profit, then the alternative plan is reduced to a critique — which may well be justified but is hardly radical — of capitalist market research. If they can only be sold at a loss then subsidy in some form is necessary and this demands some form of public intervention. Workers' plans are not therefore an *alternative* to state intervention and the AES.

## 5. Local Struggles

Local struggles, for example over cuts and closures, demonstrate important linkages with an overall economic strategy. Campaigns against the cuts in public services afford an ideal opportunity for shop stewards committees, trades councils, local political parties and local interest groups to come together in political struggles which can have a positive as well as defensive dimension. The objectives of such campaigns may sometimes be limited but they can draw attention to the way in which decisions about the allocation of resources are made, and to the way in which services are provided and controlled. But a weakness of many campaigns is that as long as they do not challenge the overall allocation of resources, their success only means setbacks somewhere else. If one threatened hospital ward is kept open while the budget of the Area Health Authority is not increased, then the cuts will simply have to be transferred to other services where defence is less well organised. It is important, therefore, to have an economic strategy at a national level which can provide the resources to ensure an *overall* increase in the provision of services.

Apart from situations where workers interests as such are involved, local struggles — over education or housing for instance — can initiate action which might achieve change by workers and their families as parents, local residents, young people, pensioners or tenants. The Labour movement must come to regard these issues, activities and campaigns as an integral part of its struggle. Our conception of the AES sees such struggles as a part of its demands and as a means of its fulfilment.

One quite fundamental choice for socialist planners is whether the enterprise plan is to be related to local and regional economic requirements or to sectoral requirements, and which of the two should 'control' the plan. In the Soviet Union, for example, the latter choice was made, whereas in China the local commune was chosen as the basic unit for planning purposes. In the context of workers' control and local struggles generally, this point is of more than academic importance, particularly for a transitional strategy.

Although it is conventional for formulations of the AES to stress sectoral planning procedures, there would be a number of advantages in the development of institutional forms and planning mechanisms which accorded a high priority to local and regional objectives. This does not imply a neglect of the implications of an industrial/sectoral strategy, but means that this would not dominate theory or practice.

The first advantage is that the danger of enterprise corporatism/syndicalism may more easily be avoided or reduced, if the plan for a particular enterprise is determined at least as much by the needs of the local economy as by the relevant industrial sector. (Of course this formulation oversimplifies the situation found in reality and ignores frequent overlaps between enterprise, local economy and industry.) An obvious example of the conflicts involved is a situation in which redundancies are 'painlessly' implemented by a recruitment ban and natural wastage. While the interests of the workers in the enterprise as such are not adversely affected, it may well mean that their sons' and daughters' employment prospects in that area are blighted as well as those of other potential workers.

A second advantage of planning mechnisms reflecting local/regional needs would be that struggles against closures and for new job creation tend to be conducted best via an alliance of forces, in which local authorities and local/regional trade union organisations are allowed to play a progressive role.

The implication of this approach for the concept of planning agreements is considerable. So far planning agreements have been conceived of in the context of a plan for the enterprise, to some extent related to the development of the industry, but not always related to local economic issues. What is implied by the approach described above is that the development of the enterprise would be set in relation to the requirements of the local/regional economy. In institutional terms this implies some 'local' representation on whatever body draws up the planning agreement and a procedure for resolving mismatch between local and central planning objectives.

## 6. Conclusion

The preceding discussion has sought to make clear the importance of progress towards workers' control, set in a local economic context as an integral part of the AES. The AES will fail unless it is able to inspire and inform activists and supporters at all levels in the Labour movement. For most people, including Labour movement activists, economic policy is something distant which does not impinge on their daily lives, while the state which implements these policies centrally, or even locally, is often seen as faceless and external. Rectifying this failing, which is not confined to capitalist economies, raises many difficult problems of how to make the institutions of the state more democratic, how they can be 'socialised', and how eventually society's needs may be expressed and satisfied in democratic ways.

In the development of planning suggested by the AES, the involvement of workers at the point of production, and of workers and their families in localities, would enable planning to be democratised from the outset. In the last analysis democratic planning in a socialist society is the means by which the key decisions are made as to the content of economic and social life. Nothing less than full democratic planning must be the objective of socialism, and hence of an alternative strategy which presents itself as a transitional step towards that goal.

# The Case for Planned Trade

## 1. Introduction

In the last five years the call for import controls has gathered strength both in the Labour movement and outside it. Individual trade unions have pressed for selective protection of industries in which the jobs of their members are threatened; the TUC has called for action by the government to stop import penetration rising in 'core' industries. The Cambridge Economic Policy Group has made a high and rising tariff on imports of manufactured goods the centre-piece of their macro-economic policy for expansion. Manufacturers too, through trade associations and Sector Working Parties, have urged the government to restrict imports of products which are undercutting the prices of their own goods—either on the grounds that imports are being 'dumped' at unrealistic prices or that they are disrupting' home markets.

The AES is clearly identified with the call for import controls. In fact, critics often characterise the AES simply as a proposal for a 'siege economy'—usually with the tag 'on the East European model'. But it should be clear from the range of sources from which the proposals are advanced that many different justifications are provided for the introduction of controls, and there are many differences between the forms of control envisaged. The call for controls in general terms is compatible with many different political positions so that it is all the more important to develop and clarify a socialist view of trade policy.

It is useful to start by looking at the problems to which pressure for import controls is a response. The British economy is highly integrated into the world economy through trade, and has been forced to undergo major structural changes as the imperialist trading relations, on which the economy was built up, disintegrated. We continue to be dependent on trade for export markets as well as for imports of food and raw materials, yet our trading position has deteriorated, at a rate which appears to have accelerated since we joined the EEC in 1973. Our export surplus in trade in manufactured goods has been eliminated and the rapid rise in imports which has brought this about is reflected in rising levels of import penetration – in some areas such as motorcycles, leading to the virtual destruction of key sectors of manufacturing industry. The weakness of our trading position has been an important factor helping to make the Balance of Payments a constraint on the expansion of the domestic economy – a constraint which obsessed policy makers in the sixties but which has been eclipsed by inflation in the seventies. In the eighties two new developments have modified the picture – North Sea oil production will have reached peak levels of production in the next few years, while the adoption of monetarist policies by the government entails a commitment to maintain the pound at a level which makes it virtually impossible for domestic producers to compete in sectors where price is the main factor in competition . In short, long-term adverse trends are being severely exacerbated by current policies.

In the framework of the AES two kinds of questions arise. The first is whether the economy can be expanded without precipitating a Balance of Payments crisis as imports rise to meet the additional demand in the economy. The second question concerns the relation between trade policy and industrial planning. We argue first that a general system of controls on the rate of growth of manufactured imports would be indispensable to allow sustained expansion; but second, that although at present demands for selective protection are primarily defensive, a broader system of selective trade controls should be developed as an essential adjunct to industrial planning. In other words we argue for planned trade within an AES.

Opposition to import controls comes not only from the Right, but also from many socialists who feel that support for import controls involves making concessions to chauvinist sentiments at the expense of socialist internationalism. We discuss below questions of internationalism and the special problem of access for developing countries' exports and make some attempt to deal with the issue of retaliation and international treaty constraints. Broadly we argue that underlying the opposition from the Right lies a firm belief in the importance of the operation of market forces at an international level expressed in the ideology of free trade. The appropriate response from socialists is to develop policies to achieve a significant degree of social control of Capital at a national level and to work for international co-operation to develop new relations in trade, industry and finance.

We now move on to consider in more detail the pattern of Britain's trade, spelling out these arguments and discussing the kind of trade policy which needs to be developed within an AES.

## 2. The Pattern Of Britain's Trade

A glance at the statistics shows that Britain is heavily dependent on international trade:

* Exports of goods and services are equivalent to nearly one third of total final output of goods in the UK.
* In the manufactured goods sector, exports again amount to a third of net output.
* About one half of foodstuffs consumed in the UK are imported.
* Britain's industry is dependent on imports of a number of raw materials that are not available or are non-economic from domestic sources.
* 21p in every pound spent by consumers in the UK goes eventually on imported goods.

The British economy is more closely integrated through trade, more 'open', than most industrialised countries, as the following figures show.

*Table 8.1: Export of Goods as Proportion of GDP (1979)*

| UK | 26.5% |
|---------|-------|
| Germany | 22.5% |
| Italy | 22.5% |
| Japan | 10.2% |
| US | 7.7% |

As a result of this openness, production and consumption in Britain have developed in response to world market forces. Whether or not such a situation is considered desirable, it would appear to be a fact that the interests of many workers in the UK are tied to the success or failure of British companies in export markets, while the interests of the consumer are tied to the availability and price of a range of goods which are traditionally imported. It is the importance of trade in the economy which has made adjustments to our changing position in the world economy all the more difficult. In recent years attention has focussed on trade in manufactured goods because export of these provides 80% of our visible exports, 60% of our total exports of goods and services and over 50% of our total current receipts of foreign currency. The main features of our declining trade position are indicated below.

* The UK share of world trade in manufactures has declined steeply—the UK's share of the world market in manufactured goods fell steadily from 24.6% in 1950 to below 9% in 1974. It has since stabilised at between 9 and 10%.

Since 1970 the volume of manufactured exports has grown by 48%—while the volume of manufactured imports has grown by 141%. The result is that the surplus in manufactured trade which has traditionally financed our imports of raw materials and food has steadily been eroded—our exports exceeded imports by 100% in 1963, by 50% in 1970 and by a mere 5% in 1979.

* The consequence of the boom in imports noted above is that 'import penetration'—the share of home markets taken by goods from overseas—has rapidly increased. In 1970 imports took 17% of the home market, and in 1979, 26%.

Table 8.2 below shows how in certain sectors the rise in import penetration has been much more rapid.

---

*Table 8.2: Import Penetration by Industry Group*

### Imports as a percentage of Home Demand

| Sector (SIC Order) | | 1968 | 1979 | Increase in Import Penetration (Percentage Points) |
|---|---|---|---|---|
| XI | Vehicles | 14 | 40 | 26 |
| | | 30 | 56 | 26 |
| IX | Electrical Engineering | 14 | 38 | 20 |
| XIV | Leather/Leather Goods | 21 | 40 | 19 |
| XV | Clothing & Footwear | 12 | 30 | 18 |
| XIII | Textiles | 16 | 33 | 17 |
| V | Chemicals & Allied Industries | 18 | 30 | 12 |
| VII | Mechanical Engineering | 20 | 32 | 12 |
| | Total Manufacturing | 17 | 26 | 9 |

---

It should be remembered however that the focus on the balance of visible trade is only a recent development. In fact for the 120 years ending with the Second World War we were quite happy to run a large deficit on visible trade financed by massive earnings on overseas investments and earnings on visible trade. When the balance of visible trade showed a small surplus in 1956, this was the first time this had happened since 1822; and when there was a massive deficit as a result of the oil price rise in 1974, the deficit was no greater in relation to National Income than it had been throughout the nineteenth century. In 1900, for example, a deficit on merchandise trade equal to 10% of National Income was offset by overseas investment earnings equal to 6% of National Income and other invisible earnings of a similar amount. The visible trade deficit in 1974 by comparison was equal to 8% of National Income. These figures are just one indication of the way in which Britain's trade 'problems' are a reflection of the country's decline as an imperial power.

In the seventies two developments made the situation worse. The first was the near four-fold increase in the oil import bill following the OPEC price rise in 1973 which left Britain with a huge deficit in trade in oil (see Table 8.3). Although the Government initially sought to live with this deficit and encourage international recycling of the surpluses built up by the OPEC countries, by 1976 this strategy had been abandoned and trade deficits and the consequent weakness of the pound were used as reasons for domestic deflation. This problem has now been reversed by the fact that Britain is now a net *exporter* of oil

The second development was Britain's entry into the EEC in 1973. This was followed by the opening up of a large deficit in trade particularly in manufacturing and particularly with Germany, France and Italy. As can be seen from Table 8.3, this made a large contribution to the overall deficit.

The imbalance in trade with the EEC points to a key factor in explaining the overall pattern of Britain's trade. The British economy, as we argued in Chapter 3, is heavily dominated by large companies with operations in many different countries. Nowhere is this dominance more clear than in the field of trade. A survey carried out by the Department of Trade in 1977 found that the top 80 exporters accounted for over three-fifths of our exports of manufactures and the top 330 companies for 86%. Among these top exporters 94% were multi-national companies and 36% were foreign controlled. Moreover a large proportion —nearly a third—of total exports of manufactures took the form of transfers between branches of the same multi-national company There are no corresponding figures for imports, but a recent study in the United States found that over half the imports of manufactured goods took the form of international transfers.

---

*Table 8.3: The Balance of UK Visible Trade 1968-79*
(£ million)[1]

|  | Balance of Trade in Oil | Balance of Trade excluding Oil | Total Balance of Visible Trade | Balance of Trade with the EEC |
|---|---|---|---|---|
| 1968 |  |  | − 712 | −251 |
| 1969 |  |  | − 209 | − 74 |
| 1970 | − 496 | + 464 | − 32 | + 39 |
| 1971 | − 691 | + 881 | + 190 | −191 |
| 1972 | − 666 | − 95 | − 761 | −591 |
|  |  |  |  |  |
| 1973[2] | − 941 | − 1645 | −2586 | −1191 |
| 1974 | −3357 | − 1993 | −5350 | −2042 |
| 1975 | −3057 | − 276 | −3333 | −2412 |
| 1976 | −3947 | + 36 | −3911 | −2127 |
| 1977 | −2771 | + 532 | −2239 | −1733 |
| 1978 | −1999 | + 506 | −1493 | −2247 |
| 1979 | − 780 | − 2532 | −3312 |  |

[1] All figures are on a Balance of Payments basis. Source: *British Business* 21 March 1980
[2] EEC entry.

---

Thus the pattern of trade is to a large extent dependent on decisions by these companies as to where to site their production, where to buy their components, and whether they supply markets by trade or by producing in those markets. The evidence is that the multi-nationals have seen Britain as a valuable *market* but not as a production base. For example, a survey of the investment intentions of UK multi-nationals after Britain joined the EEC concluded that:

· UK companies are planning to service their new or expanded European markets mainly from continental bases. This, when coupled with the evidence that continental firms are servicing their UK markets more through exports than from production facilities in the UK, is somewhat discouraging for the future growth of the UK economy." (Houston, T. and Dunning, J. N. '*UK Industry Abroad*' 1976).

And, we may add, for the pattern of trade between the UK and the EEC. We return to the question of the multi-national integration of industry and its implications below.

## 3. Expansion With Planned Trade Growth

We have outlined above the nature of Britain's dependence on trade and indicated the way in which our trading position has deteriorated in recent years. We will consider below the effects this has had in particular sectors but we begin by looking at the way the Balance of Payments acts as a constraint on the economy as a whole, and the way it could pose a serious threat to the viability of a strategy for expansion.

As the economy expands, a certain proportion of any additional spending will go on imports, either as raw materials to allow extra production, capital goods to allow investment, or finished consumer goods. Meanwhile, unless countries overseas are expanding their economies, there is unlikely to be much growth in exports. Higher levels of production may reduce costs allowing export prices to be reduced, but on the other hand higher levels of profitability in the domestic market may attract resources away from export production

The key problem has been that as home demand expands, imports (particularly of manufactured goods) have risen by a far greater proportion—roughly a 1% increase in demand has brought a 4% increase in the volume of manufactured imports. Our 'propensity to import' or 'income elasticity of demand for imports' appears to be far higher than the corresponding propensity of other countries to take our exports. For example in 1979, following an expansion of consumer demand, the volume of imports of manufactures grew by 20% while exports, and domestic manufacturing production, did not grow at all.

There are a number of reasons why this has occurred. It could be seen as part of a general process of trade liberalisation which began at the end of the fifties and has increased the share of trade in the economies of all countries. It is not our import propensities as such which are out of line (although our centralised retail network makes it relatively easy to penetrate our markets), so much as our ability to export. We are generally trapped in exports of traditional goods with low value added and low technology input—and these are precisely the markets which have not expanded. This is compounded by a failure to devote resources to marketing overseas and a greater willingness to invest abroad rather than export from the UK.

In other words the peculiar way in which we are locked into the international economic system has led to the Balance of Payments being an effective constraint on expansion to maintain full employment in the UK—a constraint which produced the stop-go policies in the fifties and early sixties and has been the excuse for deflationary policies since then. Any alternative economic strategy must include measures to deal with this problem, in the short term by controlling the surge in imports which could occur, and in the longer term by restricting our international integration.

Before looking at how imports can be controlled, this statement has to be qualified in two ways. First, just as we argue that the 'fight against inflation' has been used in recent years as the rallying cry for policies designed to undermine the strength of organised Labour, so the Balance of Payments constraint has been used in the same way in the past. Until fixed exchange rates were abandoned in 1972 the first evidence of the inflationary consequences of conflict over distribution was a decline in the competitive position of industry. A series of anti-union policies—the wage freeze in 1966 and the unsuccessful 'In Place of Strife' in 1969 for example—were introduced allegedly to correct the Balance of Payments. Any alternative strategy which saw the trade balance as the *main* constraint without understanding the political obstacles to full employment which are now centred on the 'problem' of inflation would be dangerously naive.

Second, some may suggest that with North Sea oil the problem no longer exists. This would be a mistake because although oil production obviously relaxes the constraint, it must be remembered that we are now nearing peak production and there is no evidence of a huge current surplus. In fact in 1979 there was a deficit on visible trade of over £3,000 million.

How then do we deal with the problem of imports in an expansion? There are three broad approaches. The first is to use the market; that is to adjust the level of the pound downwards in order to make imports more expensive and exports cheaper. The evidence suggests however that such a 'depreciation' or devaluation of the pound would be relatively ineffective. Again using very rough figures we find that a 2% depreciation achieves a 1% fall in the volume of imported manufactures. In other words a massive devaluation of some 15-20% would be necessary to offset the stimulus to imports of a 4% expansion of home demand.

The price mechanism in fact is not an effective regulator of international trade. There are a number of reasons for this. First, import prices tend to get built fairly quickly into wage claims so that the 'income effect' of higher import prices on living standards is offset. Prices of domestic goods then rise offsetting the 'substitution effect' arising from the relatively lower prices of home-produced goods. But the key factor is the response of large companies, which may decide to take the shift in exchange rates in higher profits (if they are exporters) or lower profits (if they are importers) rather than adjusting prices in the market in which their goods are sold. Moreover, that proportion of trade which takes the form of internal transfers is to an extent insulated from price movements. This is not to say that devaluation has no effect on the behaviour of MNCs: such companies are known to be highly sensitive to exchange rate changes in determining where to keep liquid funds, in which currencies to issue debt, and other financial questions.

It is sometimes argued that the 1967 devaluation of the pound sterling 'worked' and that arguments against devaluation (and by implication for other measures) are exaggerated. The point to be made here is that the 1967 devaluation 'worked' thanks to severe deflationary measures taken in 1968 and 1969 which raised unemployment in Britain to what was then a post-war peak of around 700,000. In the context of a demand for reflation, for increased output and reduced unemployment, we cannot seriously rely on devaluation to keep the Balance of Payments in equilibrium. This does not mean that it will be sensible to ignore the level of the pound or to maintain it at the level it is as when the Tories have office. As we argue below the present level is grossly overvalued.

Thus we would argue that more intervention in trade would be necessary but there are different ways of doing this. The second approach to controlling the Balance of Payments is to use greater discrimination in adjusting the market, by raising the price of imports (or certain groups of imports) using tariffs. This is the market oriented approach which has been advocated most notably by the Cambridge Economic Policy Group. It has proposed the implementation of a tariff on finished manufactured goods of 30% *2* (and lower tariffs on other imports) which they say may have to rise to 70% by 1990, if imports are to be kept under control while the economy expands.

This approach has great strengths in recognising the need for firm action on trade in order to achieve sustained expansion for full employment. It also makes the important point that import control need not be simply protectionist but can be used to control the *rate of growth* of imports in order to allow output to expand to provide employment. Finally it allows for the use of tariffs to give preferences to countries which are themselves in deficit, and to developing countries. But we would suggest that the Cambridge Group's formulation suffers from two weaknesses which point to broader problems. The first is an over-emphasis on the Balance of Payments constraint which leads to a view of import controls as a universal panacea. This weakness is compounded by pessimistic (though quite possibly realistic) assumptions about the demand for imports without controls, which could lead to the recommendation of extremely high tariffs. These would provide a large proportion of Government revenues after some time, so that income taxes could be reduced. But this implies substantial reductions in real gross wages (as import prices rise) which are only later compensated for by rising real net wages (as the economy grows and taxes are reduced). Yet a central theme of their analysis of the economy is the 'surprisingly stable long-term trend' in the real (gross) value of wage settlements. The second weakness is a reluctance to go beyond macroeconomic aggregates to look at the implications for industry and the kind of industrial policies which would be necessary. We would certainly agree that a framework of sustained expansion would be a necessary condition for successful industrial regeneration, but we would see it as far from sufficient.

The third approach to the Balance of Payments is to take greater direct control over the pattern of trade, controlling the volume of imports through quotas or through rationing the supply of foreign exchange. This final step away from the operation of the market is one which is often firmly resisted by many who see the necessity for some control on trade. It allows greater selectivity of control by product as well as discrimination by country.

Our argument is that without direct controls in some form on the rate of growth of imports, reflation could not be sustained and one of the main component parts of the AES would have to be curtailed or abandoned.

## 4. Planned Trade And Industrial Strategy.

We have so far considered the case for planned trade only in relation to the overall level of imports and the Balance of Payments constraint on expansion. But the pressure for import controls often stems from far more pressing concerns with the loss of jobs resulting from the rising import penetration in stagnant markets.

It is useful to distinguish two kinds of argument. The first is straightforward protectionism – foreign products are undercutting home production and should be kept out to allow domestic jobs (and profits) to be sustained. One of the major reasons why this problem is so pressing at the moment is that a major element of the Tory monetarist strategy is that high interest rates should attract money from overseas, keeping the pound high to reduce the cost of imports. Coming on top of the upward pressure on the pound from North Sea oil this has meant a disastrous fall in competitiveness, as the pound rises despite our relatively high rate of inflation. In the Tories' first year competitiveness fell by over 30%. Seen in this light pressure for import controls is a desperate defensive response to monetarism, and as long as monetarism itself cannot be challenged it seems right to support import controls – or any other measure to defend jobs – but clearly as a 'second-best' option.

There is a different kind of argument which is not related to the immediate situation but to the long-term decline of industry. It could be called the 'geriatric industry' variant of the traditional 'infant industry' argument for protection. The argument is that industry suffers from chronic underinvestment and that a 'breathing space' is necessary in order to allow investment to take place so that we can raise our productivity and so compete internationally. Protection would be necessary until costs of production declined to reach world level.

Both these arguments make the case for selective protection. In neither case, it should be noted, are the macro-economic policies assumed to change or the political constraints on expansion challenged. The second argument differs from the first in implying a clear connection with associated industrial policies to ensure that a rise in investment takes place.

Variants of these arguments are to be found in each proposal for import controls. It is worth looking in a little detail at the TUC's proposals because they represent a sophisticated development of the 'selective controls' case. Briefly they argue for a detailed industry by industry approach to controlling import penetration based on the work of the tripartite Sector Working Parties (SWPs) operating under the National Economic Development Office. This should focus on 'core' industries, defined as those producing basic industrial materials, those producing manufactured products which are essential to the production of finished goods, and finally major producers of finished goods themselves. (We suspect that this definition is sufficiently elastic to accomodate virtually any sector feeling in need of protection.)

In these core industries there would be a procedure for identifying increases in import penetration which 'threaten' UK output and employment and a range of measures should be used to check and reduce penetration. These measures would include action by government such as negotiation of voluntary export restraints, imposition of quotas and the use of public purchasing agreements. Selective financial assistance could be used to encourage the purchase of UK equipment. In addition the SWPs could make efforts to encourage communication between producers, users and consumers, and agreements could be negotiated with multi-nationals on matters such as plant location, intra-firm trade and UK-produced component content.

This approach is based on the view that countries overseas are increasingly involved in 'managing' trade, using open and hidden barriers, and on the pragmatic assessment that it is easier to play this game than openly challenge the rules of the General Agreement on Tariffs and Trade by declaring openly the intention to plan trade as part of industrial planning. For example it has been estimated that between 1974 and 1979 the proportion of trade in manufactures that was 'managed' by governments in the OECD countries rose from 4% to 15%.

We would argue that there is a clear case for using trade controls as a support to industrial planning within an AES but that this should not be confined to the 'geriatric industry' case, and that a much clearer idea needs to be developed of the *kind* of industrial structure we would be seeking to achieve through industrial planning. We would envisage trade being controlled to allow the planned run-down of industries rather than precipitate closures forced by the market, as well as protection for industries with a long-term future.

There is moreover a common presupposition which is seldom challenged on the Left or the Right, that any protection should be temporary so as to allow the domestic economic structure to be tailored to suit the requirements of the international market. It is an element of the political outlook which sees capitalism as basically efficient in managing production and in generating and channelling investment and responding to the needs of consumers, yet producing inequality and macro imbalances. These defects could be cured, so it argued, by appropriate forms of state intervention while leaving the business of production in the long run to the market and private Capital.

We return to this question in relation to the operation of multi-nationals below but here we would suggest that the case for controls on imports and exports must be argued as part of the move to take control of economic forces and reduce the power of the capitalist market over production and employment, as a necessary and permanent feature of an economy subject to democratic planning.

## 5. The Implications Of Import Controls – For Socialists And Non-Socialists

As we noted above, import controls – in whatever form – are regarded with deep suspicion and hostility by many on both the Left and the Right. To understand this suspicion, to meet some of the objections, and to try to develop a socialist position on trade planning, it is helpful to begin by looking at the basis of the strength of the ideology of 'free trade' on the Right.

Why is the option of controlling trade so strenuously shunned or opposed, both by Tories (who might have been expected to display some sentimental attachment to protectionism) and by the Right-wing leadership of the Parliamentary Labour Party? This is a fascinating question but one to which here we can only offer a few clues. The answer must start by considering how the post-war world economy was reorganised in the early 1940s. The main factor in this reorganisation was the rise to hegemonic status of the United States. The interests of capitalism within any individual country became dependent on the ability of the US to maintain or extend capitalism at the international level. Thus the various national bourgeoisies were compelled to accept the system and rules that were established by the US, and which became written into the constitution of the GATT and the IMF. To opt out was to challenge the interests and might of the US and to bite the hand that, so far as the national bourgeoisies of the European states were concerned, protected them. The Tory Party quickly appreciated this situation. The Labour movement was always more reluctant to do so, and this accounts for the extensive efforts by the US to penetrate the organisations of the European Labour movement in the late 1940s and early 1950s and, under the cover of Cold War slogans, to work against the emergence of opinion which favoured greater national autonomy in economic policy. The full facts concerning the extent to which the Labour Party and the British trade unions were penetrated by US intelligence have yet to be uncovered.

How, then, within the rules regulating the international order, were countries supposed to adjust their economies if they could not balance their international trade and payments? It soon became accepted that of the countries in imbalance, it was those with a *deficit* that were expected to adjust their economic policies; there was little pressure on the countries in surplus to make any adjustments. Countries in deficit could follow two lines of policy: deflate their economy, reduce output and employment and therefore reduce imports, or devalue. The usual first choice was deflation to regulate the inflationary pressures we have identified as stemming from conflicts over distribution.

For countries in 'fundamental disequilibrium' the remedy was devaluation which would, in theory, have the effect of reducing consumption of imports and encouraging producers and consumers to purchase from domestic sources, and of encouraging exports. Devaluation was permitted under the rules of the IMF, because it operated through the price mechanism rather than against it, and left intact the market relationships between producers and consumers. It did not involve interference with or substitution of market relationships that would have been entailed by the main alternative to devaluation: trade controls.

The socialisation of control of Capital through intervention by the nation state has always constituted a threat to Capital within the advanced capitalist countries of Europe, and it is the appreciation of this threat that lies behind bourgeois support for a system of international trade and finance that makes domestic policies and objectives subservient to and contingent upon trading performance. Unlike the 1930s and 1940s *internationalism has been adopted as a slogan of international Capital*, a situation that has caused considerable confusion among the ranks of the Left.

The basis of the liberal trading order has since the mid-seventies however been undermined by recession. In the face of stagnant markets there are strong pressures on individual governments to intervene to favour domestically-based industries. This is accompanied however by a real fear that this may lead to restricted access to markets overseas in retaliation. The result is a tentative and uneven shift towards protection — a 'new mercantilism — and attempts to manage markets at an international level, for example through the EEC's 'Davignon Plan' for steel.

How can we develop a socialist position on trade within an AES in the face of these developments? We can approach this question by responding to some of the objections to import controls which socialists often raise. The first is that they 'export unemployment'. This objection is simply misconceived. We have argued above that planned trade growth in a framework of expansion could well be the only way of increasing trade, and that there is no great virtue in succumbing to the dictates of market forces at an international level. Any other means of regulating the Balance of Payments seeks to control the level of imports by raising unemployment at home (which should be unacceptable) or by using the price mechanism alone (which is ineffective). The second kind of objection is that import controls would 'cut workers' living standards' because the price of imports would go up and people would be forced to buy more expensive domestically-produced goods. This may make some sense as a criticism of controls on their own but is nonsense within the framework of an AES designed to increase output precisely so that living standards can be increased.

Third it is suggested that retaliation would leave us worse off as our export sales were cut. This is a danger which has to be faced up to because any move towards socialism in Britain would entail a more or less radical break with the 'rules' of the international trading system: of the EEC, of the GATT and of the IMF. The problem is not confined to an import controls strategy. One response is to argue, as the Cambridge Group does, that it wouldn't be *rational* to retaliate because we would not be cutting our imports, and that by suitably interpreting the treaties (particularly using Article XII of the GATT) we could justify our position *within* those treaties. We suspect, however, that any challenge to the capitalist international order would be recognised for what it was, and would be met with appropriate disruptive response. One avenue to pursue would be the negotiation of bilateral and multilateral trade deals with other countries which have suffered from the international trading system in the same way that we have. A second is to campaign for international agreement among socialists on the need for a new system of regulation of trade which allows us to move collectively away from the policies of competitive deflation encouraged by the present regime.

Finally, there is justified concern as to the impact of controls on the developing countries. This is partly because developing countries, and particularly the Newly Industrialising Countries (NICs), are often seen as threatening to flood our markets with cheap consumer goods, and partly because the weakness of developing countries in international institutions allows them to be discriminated against more easily in trading arrangements. The first problem has to be put into perspective. Imports of manufactured goods from the NICs represent less than 10% of our total imports of these goods and this proportion has not risen in the last 20 years; moreover we have a large surplus in manufactured trade with these countries. There are a number of sectors, notably clothing, in which the NICs have substantially increased their share of the market, but overall the main threat has come from Europe, Japan and the US rather than the NICs. Second, it is certainly true that NICs suffer discrimination. The Multi-Fibre Arrangement (MFA), for example, which governs textile trade, is directed at controlling the volume of exports from 'low cost countries'. But we would argue that, subject to two qualifications noted below, a policy of planned trade would assist Third World development and would certainly be an improvement on the current recession.

The first qualification is that we would question the desirability of exporting to industrialised countries as a long-term strategy for economic development of underdeveloped countries. To some extent this strategy has been forced on underdeveloped countries by their total dependence on the financial system of the developed. It is a strategy that has numerous disturbing effects on the form of development. The second qualification is that a new strategy is emerging within the multi-nationals of shifting production out of the Western industrialised countries into Eastern Europe (where more pliable labour is available) and into so-called 'export platforms' in the Third World. There are thought to be around 200 such bases where workers are paid as little as 30 cents an hour (as in Sri Lanka) and where safety regulations and trade unionism are rare. Whether preferential access should be used to exercise leverage on the operation of such multi-nationals, is a very difficult question.

In brief, therefore, we believe that it is quite inadequate to counterpose an abstract socialist 'internationalism' to the call for the control of trade. The result is merely to give unwilling support to the case for free trade which, we have argued, operated at the expense of the working class. We have to work out in much more detail how progress can be made toward planning of trade on a socialist basis.

# The AES and International Political Economy

## 1. Introduction

In the previous chapter we argued that the ways in which Britain was integrated into the world economy through trade pointed to a number of areas of policy that would have to be developed within a comprehensive alternative strategy, and to a number of limitations that would be imposed on that strategy. We argued for going beyond the case for general import controls to protect the Balance of Payments, or selective controls to protect sectors of industry in difficulty, to develop from these a case for planning of trade. In this chapter we extend these arguments by looking at the forms of international integration and dependence through industry and through finance, and the implications these have for the AES.

To a far greater extent than most capitalist countries Britain is tied into the world economy through UK- and foreign-based multi-national companies, which have a dominant interest in the economy, and through the pivotal role played by the City of London in international flows of capital. In Chapter 3 we argued that the ways Britain is tied into the system were an important cause of the weakness of British industrial capitalism. The AES must therefore seek ways of restructuring this international dependence; at the same time it will be subject to the constraints which this dependence imposes. We look below at ways in which greater control can be exercised over multi-national companies (MNCs) through planning agreements and controls over international investment, and at ways of controlling international flows of capital.

A useful way of classifying the forms of dependence is in terms of circuits of capital operating at an international level. Capital begins as money or, more generally, as financial assets which can be used to buy machines and labour power to employ in a production process, the outcome of which is goods or commodities which, to complete the circuit, are sold for money. Capital passes through the forms of financial, industrial and commodity capital before re-appearing as finance. In modern capitalism these circuits are extensively 'internationalised' or spread across national boundaries — finance has moved with increasing freedom as exchange controls have been dismantled. Industrial production is to a great extent organised across, rather than within, national boundaries, and exchange of commodity capital or trade has for long been established but only recently liberalised. We must look at the circuits in more detail to understand the nature of the internationalisation of British capitalism and the consequences for an AES.

If we are considering an economic strategy which focuses upon a set of policies to be implemented in one country, drawing upon the mobilised strength of the working class in one nation state, we must understand the problems, and the constraints, which stem from that country's interdependence with other countries. We should also examine the support that could be expected to come from the Labour movement abroad for a country making a serious attempt to implement a transitional socialist strategy. It would be unwise and potentially disastrous to ignore both the sources of strength, and the limitations, which derive from the reality of economic interdependence. But we also have a second concern in formulating demands in relation to the international economy: to seek to determine the basis on which a just, more stable and more democratic structure can be developed at the international level — a socialist basis for economic relations between countries.

## 2. Britain And The Multi-Nationals

A multi-national company (MNC) is a company with significant production facilities in more than one country. There are few advanced industrial economies so dependent upon the MNCs as the British economy. This can be brought out in a number of ways:
* In 1971 the stock of foreign direct investment (i.e. assets owned by MNCs) by MNCs based in the UK stood at 24 billion dollars. This was more than twice that of French-based MNCs and more than three times that of German- or Swiss-based MNCs. It is exceeded only by that of US-based MNCs (assets in 1971, 86 billion dollars).
* The importance of UK-based MNCs is illustrated by the fact that the international production of these companies equalled 39.5% of *all* goods and services produced in the UK, and exceeded comfortably the output of manufacturing industry located in the UK.
* If we consider two examples: the overseas production of Unilever is 2½ times its home production and 21 times its exports from

the UK. The overseas production of ICI is 57% of its home production and twice the value of exports from the UK.
* Unilever, British-American Tobacco, Dunlop, Bowater, Beecham,
  EMI, BOC and Reckitt and Colman are UK MNCs which produce
  more overseas than they do in the UK.
* Non-British-based MNCs are responsible for a growing portion of
  manufacturing production in the UK and a growing share of UK
  markets.

In addition the multi-nationals are overwhelmingly dominant in
the field of trade, as we showed in the previous chapter. A survey by
the Department of Trade in 1976 found that 80% of the exports
covered by the sample were made by enterprises with international
connections.

What are the consequences for economic performance and for
economic strategy? The conclusion of a recent study published by
the Bank of England is worth quoting at length.

' . . .the real significance of multi-national firms is that, as they
operate internationally, they are likely to be more sensitive
than national firms to changes in the world economic environment, and consequently, to relative changes in the economic
performance of the countries in which they operate. Temporary
changes may well influence, among other factors, their decision
where to produce most of their output in the short run. The
choice is particularly important in conditions of world-wide
under-utilisation of capacity, such as those existing for most of
the 1970s. More permanent changes will influence their long-run
investment considerations, such as where to create new capacity
and where to run down or discontinue production in existing
plants. All these decisions affect output, employment and trade
performance of the industries and countries in which they
operate.'             (Panic and Joyce: 'UK Manufacturing Industry',
                      *Bank of England Quarterly Bulletin*, March
                      1980)

As firms adopt an increasingly international perspective the restructuring of production that is continually taking place under the
drive to reduce costs and maintain or increase profits may have
dramatic consequences for specific regions or even at national level.
Internationalisation of industry produces growing instability and
makes it more difficult to pursue a strategy which does not conform
to the multi-nationals' view of a stable economic and political environment within which they would like to expand.

Furthermore the existence of extensive monopoly power over the market for a whole range of vital industrial products renders obsolete the view that the economic problems of any country or region can be solved in terms of adjusting their production, their firms and their industries to the world market. That market is increasingly controlled, and entry into it protected and frustrated by the actions of existing companies. To discuss solutions to domestic economic problems without tackling the issue of how to exert social control over the activities of MNCs is to evade the central issue.

Present arrangements allow the major area of economic initiative to the MNCs. Governments have failed to develop institutions able to monitor and influence the activities of MNCs. While there has been some talk about codes of conduct for multi-nationals, arrangements for their taxation and monitoring their accountancy practices, the question of restricting the freedom of these companies in relation to disinvestment, relocation, redundancies, new investment, etc., has not been seriously considered. That the autonomy of MNCs is accepted and not challenged is evidenced by the multiple attempts by governments to compete in offering incentives, subsidies and tax holidays to encourage these companies to set up affiliates in their particular countries.

How can social control over the activities of multi-nationals be developed? In what follows we make a few suggestions, drawing upon the experience of trade unions organising around multi-nationals, but we would stress from the outset that this is an area in need of much greater attention and work by the Labour and trade union movement. The MNCs have stolen a considerable march on the Labour movement. They have fashioned forms of economic organisation over which the Labour movement has had little influence, and which have been deliberately designed so as to reduce the power of workers through their trade unions over company activities. We regard the development of multi-national capital as a serious barrier to the development of democratic and socialist forms of social control over the economy.

Before outlining a few lines of approach, we would like to make the point too that we cannot expect effective measures to come other than through organised pressure by the Labour and trade union movement. Significant opposition to MNCs now comes only from the Left: we do not foresee any significant opposition coming from either the social-democratic centre-left, the centralist liberal reformers, or the Tory Right. Right-wing nationalism in Europe has lost its material base in nationally-oriented capital. The centre and centre-left, far from representing a source of opposition, give the clearest political expression to the social ideas (ideology) that serve and express the interests of multi-national capital: a banal materialist consumerism, an 'internationalism' which reduces other nations and cultures to subservience and interprets their subjection and penetration as 'aid' and 'development', and favours soft forms of control over Labour (incomes policies and bureaucratic control over state industry and welfare, to cite a few examples).

The impact of multi-national capital upon the working class is not however identical for all sections of the class. Its negative effects are felt most by those who are made unemployed, by those employed in the small business sector, many of whom are not organised in trade unions and by those who are dependent on state welfare benefits. and who find these being reduced in order to raise company profits. By contrast, some of those employed by monopoly capital see their living standards improved as surplus value is transferred to monopoly capital from other sectors of the economy, enabling these companies to afford wages increases and remain profitable at the same time. Indeed part of the strategy of multi-national capital is to divide the workforce, by, for example, promoting company unions and company bargaining to cut across the national structure of trade unions in Britain, and by their preference for national bargaining. It is precisely this national basis for Labour organisation that multi-national capital is seeking to break down, replacing it with corporate forms of organisation which may take on 'internationalist' aspects. The organisation of workers on a national basis, according to the occupation or industry in which people work, constitutes a form of class identification of the interests and aspirations of working people. As such it constitutes the recurring threat to capital's form of social control, especially in its present multi-national phase.

The above remarks suggest that an important aspect of the development of a strategy towards the MNCs will be to maintain national, occupation or industry-based forms of organisation and bargaining in the face of pressure from capital. They suggest too that an aspect of the socialist content of such a strategy must be for the more strongly organised sections of the Labour movement to take up the concerns and cause of those groups that are weakly organised and which suffer most directly the consequences of multi-national capital.

In what ways is the Labour movement organising against the multi-nationals and in what ways can an AES extend this struggle?

1  A precondition for such organisation is information on the activities and plans of the MNCs. The trade union movement has

begun to develop this information both at national level and through the international trade union organisations such as the International Trade Secretariats (ITSs), which co-ordinate unions in a given industry or group of industries, and the International Confederation of Free Trade Unions (ICFTU). At present, however, that information is patchy and sparse, having been obtained by stealth and hard work in the face of the high degree of secrecy that surrounds company planning. A certain amount of information is available, but in a form which does not filter through in great quantities to trade unions, especially to the rank and file, namely that which is published in the business and management literature. As well as developing further its existing work in publishing information on MNCs, we see as an important part of the AES the establishment at the level of the state of an overseas intelligence unit. Such a unit could be given powers to obtain information from companies operating in the home economy, and home-based companies operating abroad, on their worldwide investment, employment and production plans.

2  Under the AES the branches of multi-nationals operating in the UK would be subject to the requirement to produce *Planning Agreements*. There would thus be compulsion upon such companies to make their operations subject to the forms of greater democratic control that are envisaged for non-multi-national companies. That a government implementing a socialist economic strategy would be in a weak bargaining position in relation to these companies cannot be doubted. The multi-nationals have at their command the control of financial resources, often the monopoly of technology, and can probably count on the backing of a significant section of their workforce, particularly those in management roles. It is a problem which can only be solved by mobilising all the sanctions and incentives available.

3  As well as developing policy at the national level, the trade union movement can be expected to continue to develop its organisation and co-operation at the international level. This has been taking place for many years through the activities of the ITSs. 'Company Councils' have been developed by some ITSs to bring together representatives of trade unions involved in a particular company. In some cases trade unions have organised sympathy strikes in many countries against the same company.

## 3. International Financial Integration

The role of the City and of sterling in the international monetary system have had a number of crucial effects on the development of the British economy, some of which we discussed in Chapter 3. First the international perspectives of the City, built up in the days when London was the key financial 'entrepot' channelling surplus basically from the black colonies to the white, have conditioned the relations between the financial system and industry in Britain. The wealth of financial interests has never been tied to the health of industry. Second, the maintenance of this pivotal international role for the City imposed requirements on domestic policy-making —
a strong and stable pound, political stability, etc. Third, the freedom of movement of capital based outside Britain has been a central and much publicised constraint on policy-making. The threat of a 'run on sterling' has normally been sufficient to guide Chancellors of both parties onto the paths of financial rectitude. The 'gnomes of Zurich' have been the frequent excuse for the abandonment of social, let alone socialist, priorities. In this section we will discuss two aspects of the problem: first the danger of short-term capital movements acting to destabilise an AES and second the longer-term problems arising from overseas investment and the invisible earnings of the City.

The role of sterling as an international currency has been declining since 1918 relative to other currencies and to gold. The present system of exchange reserves is based on dollars, gold and Special Drawing Rights (SDRs) at the IMF, with Deutschmarks representing a small but growing proportion of reserves and sterling now making up about 2% of the total. Between 1939 and October 1979 the movement of capital by UK residents was strictly limited by exchange controls covering the purchase of foreign exchange for any purpose other than trade. This did not stop overseas investment (which increased enormously in the sixties and seventies) but ensured that it was largely financed by profits of subsidiaries retained abroad or by overseas borrowing. Investment abroad not financed in this way required currency bought from the Investment Dollar Pool which was fixed in size and for which a premium was paid above the normal exchange rate.

Under this regime there were three main sources of instability and speculative pressure. The first was from the so-called 'sterling balances' — sterling deposits held by overseas governments as part of their reserves, and by companies or individuals overseas for investment purposes. In 1976, for example, it was a sudden withdrawal of official sterling balances which sparked off a run on the pound. The famous sterling crisis which resulted led to the IMF loan and allowed the Bank of England and Treasury to successfully 'bounce' the Cabinet into accepting massive spending cuts.

The second source of pressure was from short-term investments overseas in financial assets – government bonds or shares – in Britain. A certain proportion of such investment will be fairly stable but some will be volatile, shifting between currencies as interest rate differentials emerge or as expectations of currency changes develop. A problem at the moment is that there have been large inflows of short-term capital attracted by the high interest rates, particularly from OPEC countries, which could just as quickly turn into outflows.

The third source of pressure was from 'leads and lags' – that is, when companies speed up or delay payments on imports and exports to take advantage of anticipated currency movements. Although nominally controlled by exchange control regulations it was particularly difficult to control this kind of behaviour when MNCs with their huge financial balances were involved. These potential outflows remain, but with the abolition of exchange controls, the sources of speculative pressure have multiplied. We can all be currency speculators by just going to the bank and buying dollars or any other currency if we think the pound is going to fall. The consequences for an AES are extremely serious because it is improbable to say the least that a strategy for expansion and planning could be implemented with the confidence of the international financial community.

The effect of a loss of confidence and a flood of sterling being offered for other currencies would be to drive down the exchange rate for sterling well below the level that would be justified by international comparisons of prices or by the balance on the trade and invisibles account. The result of this would be to worsen significantly the terms of trade, make imports much dearer and possibly make it difficult for importers to obtain goods and services at any price if there were great uncertainty about the future exchange rate. This would cause a severe dislocation to output and employment and a consequent cut in living standards. A further difficulty is that even the *possibility* of a government elected on a socialist programme could spark off a sterling crisis which could be used as a warning to the electorate by a Conservative Government.

Turning to the long-term effects of free international capital movements, we can see that a result of the abolition of exchange controls has contributed to making the external constraints upon domestic economic policy sharper and more powerful. If profitability in the UK relative to profitability overseas now falls we can expect a greater and more rapid outward flow of investment. This provides an immediate material basis for attempts to persuade workers that profits are necessary and must be increased if jobs are to be retained, that productivity must be higher, wages lower and the whole paraphernalia of bourgeois justifications for measures which enhance the accumulation of capital at the expense of the working class. Increased freedom for capital to move between countries enhances the international capitalist discipline on conditions of production and conditions of work and pay, and further limits the autonomy of national economic policy or strategy.

It should be clear that a government implementing an AES would have to take rapid steps to regain and extend control of international capital movements. It is unlikely that the Bank of England would allow the pound to fall too far, and the high current and expected levels of reserves of foreign exchange would allow it some room for manoeuvre, allowing some time for controls to be established. Although the legislation providing for exchange controls has not been abolished it may take some time to allocate staff to this work since the 400-strong unit at the Bank of England has been disbanded. There would be a case therefore for a complete suspension of convertibility for a temporary period.

Beyond that time it is a question of looking at options. One option would be to restore exchange controls on capital movements by UK residents and try to reduce the impact of overseas capital movements on the economy. One step would be to remove the overhang of sterling balances using North Sea oil revenues or liquidation of UK assets overseas. This was an important question when the AES was initially formulated in opposition to the IMF in 1976, but it may well be dwarfed by other more pressing difficulties. A second step would be to tighten up on 'leads and lags' through exchange controls. A more radical option would be a total suspension of convertibility for capital movements so as to freeze overseas investment in the UK, but this would involve a variety of costs and may allow leakages through current transactions. The final option would be to permanently suspend free convertibility of sterling so that allocation of foreign exchange for purposes of purchasing imports would be a responsibility of a body charged with the planning and direction of foreign trade. Allocations for investment purposes, or withdrawal of overseas investments in the UK, would be subject to stringent controls.

## 4. The Possibility Of A National Strategy

We have discussed the ways in which Britain is integrated into the world economy, the forms of internationalisation, and we have argued that this has conditioned economic developments in Britain and would impose serious constraints on an AES. This leads some socialists to argue that it is futile to pursue a strategy for transition at a national level. Either it is doomed to failure or it will become hideously disfigured through the identification with national interests. Below we take up these arguments and make the case for the possibility and the necessity of a national strategy, but also the need to adopt at every stage an international orientation.

In our discussion of economic crisis in Chapter 3 we argued that while the existence and necessity of crises could not be avoided while production remains organised on a capitalist basis, the form in which the crisis manifested itself and the way in which the crisis was resolved to permit a period of renewed accumulation depended crucially on the nature and extent of working-class struggle and the policies adopted by the State. This argument can be extended to the international sphere.

An important consequence of international economic integration is the instability it engenders in individual countries. The spread of multi-national capital means that employment, incomes and investment in a country become significantly affected by the decisions of a small number of companies as to where to locate new plant or to cut back existing production facilities. Freedom of capital movement, combined with the breakdown of the structure of fixed exchange rates in 1972, and the imbalances following the accumulation of massive surpluses by the OPEC countries, have increased the instability caused by massive fluctuations in exchange rates. Finally the liberalisation of trade has meant that the general level of economic activity in any one country is dependent on the general level of world output. The rules of the GATT and the IMF force countries to tailor their economic policies to the general world situation, and reduce the ability of national governments to take independent action to reduce unemployment through an expansion of demand.

In other words the internationalisation of capital in its financial, industrial and commodity form, has extended the 'market' from a national to an international level. The basis by which trade and capital are regulated at the international level, a basis enshrined in the rules of the GATT, the articles of the IMF and the Treaty of Rome, are not simply the legal aspect of a technical economic mechanism devoid of political content. The market—and today, the international market—is an essential and central ingredient of capitalist class rule and it is the freedom of capital to operate through markets that is the common thread running through the constitution of the organisations we have just cited. The market is a form of social organisation which serves the collective interests of capital. It is from this basis that we must in the final analysis evaluate socialist policies for the international economy and evaluate the opposition that they will encounter, not only from capital but also from many who claim to be opposed to capitalism.

What are the consequences of these developments at a national and international level? While continuing to keep the function of maintaining internal social order, national states have been increasingly subject to international events and pressures over which as national states they have little direct control, given their unwillingness to change the structure of rules by which international economic interdependence has been built up. The unwillingness of Labour governments to challenge these basic rules bred an attitude of fatalism and despair with regard to economic policy during the 1960s and then after 1975, symbolised in the passive acceptance of the package of economic measures imposed in 1976 as the condition for an IMF loan. Fatalism in the Labour Party has been matched by a positive enthusiasm among Tory ranks for the ideological notion of 'the laws of economic reality' which allegedly dictate that jobs living standards and public services must be reduced so that Britain can once again 'pay her way'.

But at an international level there is a contradiction between the internationalisation of capital and the continuing national basis of effective political institutions and power. This has led to the attempt to develop supranational political bodies of which the EEC is the prime example. The fundamental reason for its existence is the attempt to reduce to manageable proportions the 'relative anarchy' which would otherwise characterise the relations between the European economies. This is being done through the regulation of competition, the controlled restructuring of major industrial sectors such as steel, textiles and the motor industry, and the farm and monetary policies. It is also leading to the development of an EEC role in the monitoring and maintenance of internal social order within European countries as EEC law and administrative powers are increased.

At what level, then, can the effects of internationalisation be challenged? The greatest threat to capitalism has always come from the attempts by the working class to assert its interests against those of capitalist accumulation. This opposition has sometimes taken the form of struggle over national political objectives and policies, and in the early post-war period major advances were made by the British working class with the nationalisation of industries, the establishment of a health service and other improvements in welfare. Such demands (and achievements) were expressed through the political machinery of the *national* state. Since the post-war Labour reforms there has always been the possibility that the Labour movement would make new demands expressed through national politics that would restrict the freedom of operation or the property rights of private capital. The most general contradiction of capital remains that between its private ownership and accountability and control and the sweeping social character of its effects.

Although it has been argued that it is at the national level that the working class has been most effective in organising against capital, this does not mean that we regard as insignificant the international co-operation that has developed among workers across national frontiers. We do however believe that it will be through struggle around the policies and political institutions of the nation state that decisive political advance by the working class can be made. International organisation and co-operation should be seen in the light of the need to relate international trade union activity to the broader task of furthering socialist and democratic policies at the level of those forms of state power that are at present the decisive forms of state power, namely the nation state.

This point can be developed by looking at the question of the Common Market. The debate on the Left about the EEC should be concerned with the question of whether the developing state power represented by the EEC is best tackled by a concerted effort on the part of the European working-class movement to impose social control over this unique development in Western capitalism, or whether a concerted effort to destroy what has so far been established is the better way. Whichever of these options is chosen an international perspective and consciousness by the European working class will be important and in this respect the growing practical solidarity that has been developing through the European Trades Union Congress (ETUC) is encouraging.

What is absolutely certain is that independent action of a half-hearted kind by a part of the working-class movement in Britain based on precious little save chauvinism will simply serve to weaken solidarity in the European Labour movement and will not greatly impede progress towards capitalist integration within Western Europe.

Elements of the AES have been advocated or form part of the programme of significant forces on the European Left, such as the Socialist and Communist parties in France and Italy and in sections of the Left in Holland, West Germany and the Scandinavian countries. The AES is not in that respect confined to any particular nation, although many of its demands are expressed as policies to be implemented by nation states. The autonomy sought in national economic policy is not autonomy from or against workers in other countries, but autonomy with respect to Capital and its forms of social control.

There is therefore considerable potential for *internationalising the AES* — for developing international solidarity around the type of policy contained in the AES. It is very important for the Left not to be confused into accepting the ideology of capitalist international- ism, and counterposing to this the 'chauvinism' of a political orient- ation towards the development of national state economic policies. The correct distinction is that between social control by inter- national capital, and democratic political social control that can be developed through political institutions, be they the political instit- utions of the nation state or other focuses of democratic decision- making that we seek to develop. It is because of the continuing pol- itical significance of national state political institutions, both as the focus of an albeit limited form of political democracy and as the expression of an historical and cultural identity, that the Left should seek to develop and influence state policies.

## 5. Conclusion: A Socialist Perspective On The International Economy

The main conclusion of this chapter is that the involvement of the UK in the world economy does not present an insuperable obstacle to the implementation of an alternative economic strategy, but does entail a number of measures to be taken concerning trade, capital movements, sterling and the MNCs. The present 'rules of the game', according to which capital in its commodity or its money forms is relatively free to move across international borders, would be quite incompatible with attempts within one country to reduce significantly the autonomy and social power of capital. The adoption of a policy of controls on trade, industry and capital should not therefore be considered a purely technical matter of balancing the magnitude and composition of trade and capital flows. It must be considered as part of a concerted move to place economic processes under greater democratic control and to adapt economic resources to meeting the needs of people rather than the need to accumulate capital. As such, this policy will serve the interests of the mass of the people —the working class—and will be strongly opposed by Capital.

# Controlling Inflation

## 1. Introduction

The problem of inflation has dominated British politics over the last decade. Since Heath won the 1970 election on a promise to 'cut the rate of increase of prices at a stroke' (widely misreported as a promise to achieve an actual cut in prices) the two main parties have competed on the basis of the strength and credibility of their claims to be able to 'win the battle' against inflation. The political debate over inflation has been distorted on all sides by rhetorical appeals and misrepresentations of the real issues. Inflation has been presented as a generalised threat—the 'enemy of national welfare', the scourge of the housewife and the low paid, the exploiter of the pensioner and small saver—in order to enlist under the banner of the fight against inflation a broad range of support for policies designed in practice to curb real wages and undermine trade union rights.

The first task then is to try to identify in what sense inflation really is a 'problem'—and a problem for Labour rather than Capital. In doing this it is useful to try to distinguish between harmful consequences which can be attributed to inflation itself and those which are the result of failures of adjustment and the very policies which are introduced for the purpose of reducing inflation. Our conclusion is that going beyond the rhetoric we can identify some real damage inflicted by inflation, but we must also take into account the strong popular aversion to inflation even where we cannot find a clear material basis for it.

A viable economic strategy must include measures for controlling if not reducing inflation. In order to assess the different approaches adopted for dealing with inflation it is helpful to introduce a framework for understanding the process of inflation. We argue below that inflation is the outcome of conflicts over distribution. The accelerating inflation in most Western countries in the seventies is the classic symptom of intensified conflicts—or class struggle—in distribution and production between Capital and Labour.

Once we understand inflation in these terms rather than as something 'caused' by wage rises, by the money supply, or by monopoly profits, we can go on to see how different methods of controlling inflation seek different ways of resolving the underlying distributional conflicts. They may be resolved either 'directly' through incomes policy, anti-trade union legislation, price control, or indirectly through the market using higher unemployment, achieved either by fiscal deflation or by monetary control.

Clearly within discussion of the AES we have to face up to the related problems of the control of inflation and the determination of incomes. Unfortunately discussion of these issues on the Left has not progressed very far. There has been a peculiar paralysis of socialist thought in this area which has allowed the Right in the Labour Party and outside to set the terms of the debate. We will discuss below the roots of this situation, and argue for steps towards social rather than market determination of incomes in·a clear strategy for controlling inflation as part of a full AES. Our broad position is that any agreed restriction on the freedom to use the basic bargaining strength of the trade unions in negotiation of wages must be matched by an extension of bargaining and control over the full range of strategic decisions within the enterprise.

We now move on to spell out in detail the arguments summarised in this introduction.

## 2. In What Sense Is Inflation A Problem?

"Nothing so undermines a nation as inflation."
*Labour's Manifesto 1979*

"Inflation is our enemy because rising prices hit most hard at the pensioner, the low paid and the housewife and inflation causes loss of jobs.'
James Callaghan  *Preface to Labour's Manifesto 1979*

Inflation is quite simply a continuing rise in the general level of prices. Why should this worry people so much? Indeed worry them to the extent that both major parties can compete for votes on the basis that they will give higher priority to policies to reduce inflation. We want to show how this issue has been misrepresented, before going on to look at what we see as the real problems arising out of the impact of inflation on working people.

In order to assess the real costs of inflation it is useful to look at the most common responses to the question 'why is inflation a problem?'

1 *'Inflation reduced living standards'* Certainly if money incomes are fixed and prices rise then — other things being equal — living standards are reduced. But on the other hand, inflation is quite compatible with rising living standards as long as money wages are adjusted to rise faster than prices. It should be noted of course that even if money wages do not keep pace with price rises, inflation does not *reduce* 'national welfare' — the total of goods and services produced — but rather it redistributes command over these use values from wages to profits.

2 *'Inflation causes loss of jobs'* There are different accounts of how this is supposed to happen. *One* is simply that as domestic prices rise, UK exports become less competitive overseas and people choose to buy imports as they become relatively cheaper. This is only true though if the exchange rate fails to adjust to compensate for the differential between the rise in domestic costs and costs overseas. Depreciation of sterling is then an obvious way of countering this particular effect. A *second* account is that inflation causes 'uncertainty' which obstructs business decisions on matters such as investment. Uncertainty may arise from a number of source: uncertainty about future profit levels, about movements in costs, about movements in relative prices. But it is by no means obvious that uncertainty increases as inflation rises. Indeed it could be argued convincingly that uncertainty arises from possible *changes* in the rate of inflation and these can occur just as readily at 2% annual inflation as at 20%. Often lurking behind these arguments is a *third* account, sometimes brought out into the open, that *wage* 'inflation' causes a loss of jobs because it shifts income from profits to wages. Whether a marginal reduction in profits causes a fall in employment is debatable, but it should be made clear that shifts in distribution of this kind can take place at any level of inflation and so are not a cost attributable to inflation itself.

3 *'Rising prices hit most hard at the pensioner, the low paid and the housewife'* This statement from the preface to Labour's 1979 Manifesto seems to embody a number of common misconceptions. State pensions are at present linked to price rises or to the increase in earnings whichever is the higher so that there is no reason — provided the government is honest in making adjustments — why pensioners should be hardest hit. Furthermore, there is no evidence that the relative position of the low paid

deteriorates in times of inflation. For example, between 1973 and 1977—a period of rapid inflation—the lowest decile of male earnings rose as a percentage of the median from 65.6% to 68.1%. In the following two years—in which inflation was substantially lower—the low paid slipped back almost to the position of 1973. Finally, it is difficult to see why the housewife should suffer or gain more than any other member of the family. Obviously to the extent that women are responsible for a greater proportion of consumer expenditure (by no means proven) and earn a smaller proportion of household income they will be more conscious of price rises than the corresponding income rises which maintain their living standards. But why this means they are 'hit most hard' by rising prices is far from clear.

Two incidental points arise here. *First* it is to be hoped that the Labour Party will avoid using formulations which refer to the 'housewife'. If women are to be regarded as having equal economic status to men—without which our commitment to equal pay and equal opportunity are vitiated—then we must make efforts to break down the sexist attribution of domestic roles. *Second*, women are being invited to see themselves as housewives faced with rising prices. They are then led implicitly to see rising wages—and union activity—as the cause of rising prices rather than as a source of rising income which maintains living standards. This political approach is however an important source of support for the ideology of the Tories, and one which Labour should surely be working against rather than attempting to manipulate for its own ends.

So far the arguments we have made have been put polemically in order to highlight the need to approach discussions of inflation critically. We can now go on to assess in a more balanced way the real costs and fears underlying popular concern over inflation. There is first the fact that, in mild forms, inflation devalues, and in extreme forms, may actually destroy, the price mechanism. This is shown at its simplest in the inconvenience caused in shopping because extra information needs to be collected in order to distinguish between relative and absolute price movements. There must always be a fear too that escalating inflation may ultimately destroy the role of money as a means of exchange—the haunting vision of Weimar's wheelbarrows of Deutschmarks.

Second, inflation causes arbitrary (though systematic) redistributions. Unless nominal interest rates rise to cover the rate of price increases, lenders will suffer as the real value of the capital sum lent is eaten away. Borrowers make a corresponding gain, and since the biggest borrowers are the banks, home buyers, the government and industry, the gains are not all evenly distributed. These redistributions could be simply countered by straightforward indexation of money contracts so that any interest paid becomes a real return. There is however a further kind of redistribution. To the extent that inflation is associated with expansion of credit, it involves the creation of new command over goods and services produced in the economy, and it is important how this command is distributed. Monetarists for example have been particularly concerned that expansion of credit to finance state spending involves increasing the command of resources through the public sector, at the expense of the holders of 'money balances'. While socialists should not be too concerned with this aspect of the process, we have neglected the role of allocation of bank credit, which is heavily weighted toward middle-class occupations and activities, as an element in distribution.

The third kind of cost is that although inflation does not necessarily cut living standards it increases the *vulnerability* of real wages. It is much more difficult to defend real wages when it involves bargaining for a money wage rise above the rate of inflation, than when it means merely avoiding an actual cut in the pay packet. Moreover bargaining itself entails costs in lost wages through strikes and the like. A further point is that since wages are only adjusted every year while price rises are continuous there is a perception of living standards being constantly eroded.

Fourth there is no doubt that while UK inflation in the seventies never approached levels of 'hyper inflation', it has contributed to a general sense of instability, and a recognition of the fundamental conflicts underlying the determination of income distribution. To say that inflation need not damage competitiveness because the pound can be devalued to accommodate relative cost movements is too glib because a depreciation will mean higher import costs which will no doubt be built into higher wage claims and intensified conflict. The aversion to inflation is in a sense an aversion to social conflict, a lesson with ambivalent implications for the Left.

Finally it must be recognised that when people talk of inflation they mean different things—to put it crudely, business is basically concerned with rising wages rather than rising prices, and the possible threat to profits. Labour, on the other hand, is concerned with the threat to *real wages* from earnings rising slower than prices.

In conclusion, therefore, we have argued that it is important to try to 'demystify' the ideological presentation of the 'problem' of inflation, but at the same time to recognise the real costs underlying the widespread popular concern about its effects.

## 3 Understanding The Inflationary Process

To understand the significance of inflation and assess different approaches to controlling it, it is essential to try to build a framework for understanding what causes inflation. Debate has unfortunately been channelled into fruitless disputes as to whether rising wages are the cause of inflation, or whether they only 'cause' 40% or whatever of inflation, and that therefore unions are not to 'blame'. It is equally fruitless to dispute whether excessive monetary growth causes inflation, when no serious account is provided of the determinants of the money supply.

We must try to get away from accounts of inflation which search for a single cause and try to understand the way that inflation is generated by a system founded on conflict and subject only to indirect means of control. It is rather like asking what causes rainfall—is it the sunshine which causes evaporation from the sea? Or perhaps the gravity which prevents the raindrops moving upwards? Obviously no explanation is adequate on its own but each will be part of a more complete account. We would argue that inflation is fundamentally about conflicts over distribution, and the inflation of the seventies is the classic form of expression of this conflict in an economic system we have described as 'state-managed monopoly capitalism'.

To build up the explanatory framework it is useful to start with a highly simplified model. We look at an economy where there is no government and no trade. We also assume that there is no growth in output and that no group of workers or capitalists gain at the expense of others. The basic characteristics of the economy are:

1 It is *capitalist*. This means simply that the means of production— the factories, machines, etc.—are owned by one set of people while another set of people live by selling their labour. The output of the economy is thus divided into wages going to the labour force and profits received by the owners.

2 It is *dominated by large companies*. We use the word 'monopoly' loosely to describe an economy in which production is concentrated in sufficiently few units to allow prices to be set by companies rather than by the market. In practice this means that companies use 'mark up' pricing—setting the price to give a desired level of profits over and above costs.

How will the distribution between wages and profits be determined in such an economy? If workers were not organised collectively and there was a large pool of unemployed, then wages would be forced down to a subsistence level, leaving the output not forming part of the subsistence wage to go to profits. (Such an economy could only continue operating if profits were spent on luxury consumption or investment. Otherwise not all output would be sold.) However the existence of large units of production encourages workers to organise in pursuit of wages above subsistence.

Workers are able by forming trade unions to minimise competition among themselves and thus claim a larger share of output at the expense of profits. However, the basic problem faced by workers is that they can bargain only over money and not real wages, and that decisions on prices remain in the hands of capitalists. Thus if workers collectively were able to increase their wages in money terms through bargaining, it would be open to companies to raise prices by the same amount to cover their costs and restore the share of profits. Similarly if companies attempted to increase the share of profits by raising prices, workers would be expected to defend their real wages by demanding a corresponding money wage increase.

In this highly-simplified model, inflation might arise from a conflicting attempt by either Labour or Capital to increase its share of output. The level and persistence of inflation generated would depend on the intransigence of each side (expressed in the money wage bargain), and institutional factors such as the frequency of wage negotiations and price adjustment decisions. A crucial factor would be the bargaining power of Labour which would be dependent on such factors as the degree of trade union organisation and the level of unemployment.

To understand the inflationary processes in the real world we have first to extend the simple model to include two further sections which make claims on output: the state and the overseas sector. Introducing trade and capital movement with the overseas 'sector' raises complex questions about the possibility of inflation being carried across national boundaries. Here we will concentrate on just one issue, the effect of changes in the 'terms of trade' on inflation. The 'terms of trade' is simply a measure of the relative price of UK exports as compared to imports. If it rises the same volume of exports will buy more imports so the total income of the country will increase. If the terms of trade fall, for example as the result of rapid inflation overseas, a fall in the value of the pound, or a huge increase in the price of an important commodity like oil, then collective income is reduced. The initial impact of such a change will be on import prices but what is more important is the effect of such an initial price increase on the struggle between wages and profits. If money wages are not increased the entire burden of the shift in terms of trade will be borne by Labour. If money wage claims take into account higher import prices then an inflationary spiral is set in motion.

The present strategy among Western governments is to ensure that the costs of the latest OPEC round of oil price increases are borne by wages. This is to be achieved by higher unemployment brought about through tight monetary and fiscal policies and through—in the words of a recent OECD communique—"dialogue between or with the social partners on the need to accept the consequences of higher oil prices on real incomes". In other words incomes policy to cut real wages.

To introduce the state into the model we have to take account of the different ways in which it can intervene in the economy. *First* the state can make claims on resources through taxation. It could be argued that an important factor in inflation at the end of the sixties was that it was only in that decade that income tax became a tax on the working class. In 1960 the average tax rate for a man earning average manual wages (with a wife not earning and two children under the age of 11), was 5%. By 1970 this had increased to 15%. As long as expenditure financed in this way is not regarded as an acceptable substitute for expenditure out of personal income, workers will seek to maintain the real value of *net* (i.e. post tax) incomes. In other words increased claims by the state can initiate an inflationary spiral as Labour and Capital seek to minimise the burden placed on the share of wages or profits. Second the state can intervene in the process of distributional conflict by setting the general framework of conflict through fiscal and monetary policy, by transferring income from one sector to another through transfer payments or subsidies, or finally by intervening directly through incomes policies. Very broadly the choice faced by the state has been between intervening to hold down money wage claims or deflating the economy so as to raise unemployment and undermine trade union bargaining power. We will return to the effects of these different options for state intervention and their effects below.

Finally it is necessary to mention briefly two further factors which make the simplified model more useful. The first is growth in the economy which can help to moderate inflationary pressures because conflicts over *additional* shares of a growing product are less severe than those over absolute levels of income. The second factor is the possibility of fractional conflicts. An example would be the attempt by financial capital to claim a larger share of the surplus at the expense of the profit of industrial capital or one group of workers seeking a larger share at the expense of others.

To conclude this section we will quickly relate the framework we have outlined to the recent experience of inflation. The actual path of inflation will be heavily influenced by the relative strength of class forces. Recent years have seen a significant deepening and extension of trade union organisation, but also a continuing tendency towards concentration and internationalisation in the industrial structure, with the growth of new monopoly formations. These developments have substantially strengthened the defensive capabilities of Labour and Capital respectively, and contributed to the aggravation of inflationary conflicts, as the figures indicate.

*UK inflation % (annual average)*

| 1960-64 | 2.8 |
| 1965-69 | 4.3 |
| 1970-74 | 9.6 |
| 1975-79 | 14.1 |

Moreover, in the period since 1960, we can identify a consistent decline in the rate of growth of both productivity and national income. This process is reflected in the breakdown of the post-war settlement between Capital and Labour, in which the working-class aspirations for improved living standards and social provision were largely met out of an increasing national income and tax base. It is this gradual collapse of growth which lies at the heart of renewed inflationary crises in Britain, with the working class making demands on the resources available to Capital but which Capital is progressively less able to accept.

In the seventies these tendencies were severely exacerbated by the rise in oil prices and then paradoxically made even worse by the very policies designed to curb inflation. Although incomes policies provided a temporary disguise, the effect of deflationary policies was to increase inflationary pressures because increasing demands were made on a shrinking tax base, while growth was held back. These policies combined with cuts in the 'social wage' produced pressures for money wage claims above the rise in productivity.

In short inflation is a *process* based on conflict. The mechanisms through which this process is *sustained* may be very different from the development or event through which it was initiated. The role of trade unions in this process is to defend the share of wages in output and to defend the legitimate aspirations of the working class for rising living standards. Thus the attribution or denial of blame is futile; what is important is the source of conflict and the way it is resolved. It is to the resolution of the conflict that we now turn.

## 4. Approaches To Controlling Inflation

Using the framework developed so far we can see the problem of inflation as a symtpom of the fundamental class conflict on which capitalism is based. Approaches to 'dealing with' inflation are approaches to intervening in this conflict. We will briefly review the different forms of intervention – three normally advocated from the Right are deflation, monetary control and incomes policy, while from the Left price controls are often proposed.

*Deflation*, like monetary control, is an attempt to influence the outcome of struggle indirectly by setting the parameters of conflict against Labour. The prime concern of those who opposed, and indeed many of those who supported, the rise of the Keynesian ideology of demand management after the war, was that prolonged full employment would strengthen the bargaining power of Labour thus making either permanent inflation or permanent incomes policies inevitable, or forcing the abandonment of high employment policies. Writing in 1943, the Marxist economist Michael Kalecki foretold that:

"If attempts are made to maintain the high level of employment in the subsequent boom a strong opposition of 'business leaders' is likely to be encountered . . .lasting full employment is not at all to their liking. The workers would 'get out of hand' and the 'captains of industry' would be anxious to 'teach them a lesson'. Moreover, the price increase in the upswing is to the disadvantage of small and big rentiers. . .

"In this situation a powerful block is likely to be formed between big business and the rentier interests, and they would probably find more than one economist to declare that the situation was manifestly unsound. The pressure of all these forces, and in particular of big business – as a rule influential in government departments – would most probably induce the government to return to the orthodox policy of cutting down the budget deficit. A slump would follow. . ." (M.Kalecki, 'Political Aspects of Full Employment', *Political Quarterly* 1943)

Such a forecast proved accurate in the seventies when the goal of full employment was abandoned and the economy was deflated in the name of controlling inflation. The problem this strategy faced, however, was that the strength of organisation was such that real wage settlements were relatively insensitive to unemployment levels while deflation itself, as we suggested above, produces inflationary effects.

*Monetarism* is essentially a form of deflation which seeks to reduce the level of demand in the economy by controlling the money supply, and cutting back on public borrowing in order to help achieve this. While deflation was accompanied by attempts to control wages directly, monetarism marks a radical return to reliance on 'market forces'. It signals a loss of faith by key sections of Capital in the effectiveness of state action, and in particular its ability to achieve a solution to the inflationary crisis without a permanent change in the balance of class forces in favour of Capital. We see monetarism as a coherent body of political, economic and social initiatives, which links an anti-inflation policy to attacks on welfare spending, trade union rights and the security of employment: in other words, it explicitly recognises the class roots of the problem of inflation in capitalist society.

Unlike conventional deflation, monetarism seeks to take unemployment out of the political arena by adopting fixed rules of monetary growth. The government can claim that the monetary target is a neutral policy which only becomes deflationary if prices rise faster than the money supply. Although the logic is rather obscure, trade unions can then be accused of pricing *themselves* out of a job if they pursue wage claims above the allowed increase in money supply. Cash limits in the public sector can be used to reinforce this claim. Rather like leads with a sliding loop sometimes used to train young dogs, monetary control attempts to transfer responsibility for unemployment to the unions which find that the harder they struggle to maintain real wages the tighter the noose becomes.

*Incomes policies*, with the exception perhaps of the third stage of Heath's policy in 1973 when wages were linked to prices, have been policies of wage restraint designed to reduce the share of wages and increase the share of profits. This assertion is evidenced by the fact that between 1948 and 1976 there were fourteen years in which incomes policies were operated, and over these periods net real income of the man with two children fell by 2%. In the periods without incomes policy net real income rose by over 45%. The problem has been that incomes policies could not be sustained and real wages have tended to 'catch up' to their rising trend level as

incomes policies collapse. We return to the problem of income determination under an AES below.

*Price Controls* finally are the option generally favoured by the
Left. We believe that they would play a big part in any strategy for
controlling inflation but that it would be a mistake to see them as
sufficient in themselves. Price controls as they have been practiced
have little to do with controlling inflation because they have simply
been controls on profit margins. As long as costs are rising, control
of the mark-up over costs will not prevent inflation. Price controls
are of value in the sense that they are *not* an intervention to reduce
the shape of wages, but if price controls were to be strengthened to
control the *absolute* level of prices while costs and particularly
incomes were free to rise we would have to face up to the consequences for company profits. There are perhaps three views in the
Left as to the impact of a lower profit share:

1 there are substantial excess profits being made so that a reduction
in the share of profits would not affect the level of investment.

2 a reduction in profits would lead to a cut-back in investment and
possible bankruptcies so that the share of profits should be protected or increased.

3 a reduction in profits would lead to the effects outlined in (2) but
this is to be welcomed as a step forward toward the demise of
capitalism.

Some may welcome the elimination of profit through price
control combined with militant wage bargaining on the grounds
that the system will become unworkable and socialism will rise,
phoenix-like, from the ashes of the ensuing crisis. A far more likely
outcome, and recent experience bears this out, is that conflicts take
the form of rising inflation and falling profits which lead to popular
acceptance of the need for cuts in real wages, curbs on trade unions
etc. to deal with the 'inflationary menace'. The converse view that
surplus profit can be painlessly eliminated seems equally mistaken.
There *has* been a crisis of profitability in British industry even if
certain sectors such as oil or banking have gained large returns.
Profits are generally at historically low levels. The consequences for
profit of controlling inflation through price controls therefore must
be looked at seriously. We thus have to consider the question of the
determination of incomes.

## 5. Income Determination Under An AES

It should be clear from what we have said about the nature of the conflicts underlying inflation that we see Free Collective Bargaining (FBC) backed by the sanctions of industrial action, as the funda-mental expression of the economic strength of the organised Labour movement in these conflicts. The key point which we feel disting-uishes our discussion of the determination of incomes from Social Democratic accounts is that we see it as essential to preserve and extend, rather than to dissipate, this basic bargaining strength.

Having emphasised the value of FCB, however, we would also like to draw attention to its weaknesses as part of a socialist economic strategy. The first weakness is that when trade unions successfully exercise their basic economic strength in pursuing wage claims, and thus increase the share of wages at the expense of profits, they are faced with contradictions as long as the crucial economic decisions about prices, production and investment lie in the hands of capital-ists. Either wage increases are passed on in higher prices so that workers have to struggle once again to maintain the real wage level or, if higher costs are not passed on, profitability is reduced. This is by no means disastrous, but it will put pressure on companies to close unprofitable plants, to cut back on investment which is largely financed out of profit, and on multi-nationals to transfer production overseas. It will also provoke the kind of political attack described in Chapter 3.

Thus, Free Collective Bargaining may be the best means of defence, but in isolation it is an ineffective and contradictory weapon of attack. What is vital therefore is to translate the basic economic strength that is exercised through FCB into a broader social and political strength, while losing none of the capacity to defend.

The second reason why FCB on its own is inadequate is that bargaining can never be 'free'—it is simply subject to varying constraints. It is rather like the handcuffed prisoner in a police cell demanding to have his handcuffs removed and calling it freedom. This is true particularly in the public sector—central and local government and nationalised industries, where a third of the work-force is employed—where decisions about the level of wages are political decisions about the level of public spending. Even outside the public sector, bargaining necessarily takes place in a legal and economic environment controlled by the state.

Finally FCB is the easy subject of a number of ideological attacks. It can be condemned as the 'philosophy of the pig trough', and accused of allowing the strong to gain at the expense of the weak, and of having no regard for a more egalitarian distribution of income. In fact of course, during periods of incomes policy, the better-off usually improve their position relatively since white-collar workers find it easier to evade wage controls. But nonetheless attacks of this kind allow public opinion to be turned against the trade union movement. Moreover it is a strategy based on the market determination of incomes. It can lead to heightened distributional conflicts *within* the working class and thus to a degree of disunity.

We have set out the strengths and limitations of free bargaining in general terms, but we should be clear that the difficulties we have identified will be particularly acute in the context of an AES. First the AES would follow a period of sustained and acute crises in the capitalist order, characterised by severe downward pressure on working-class living standards. Experience of formal incomes policies suggests that this is a period when the aspirations for wage increases are considerably heightened. Of course, it is part of the AES that reflationary action by the state would provide scope for early increases in living standards, but the speed of reflation would be constrained by the state of the economy and by supply bottlenecks. Moreover, a substantial portion of increased output would be claimed by those initially unemployed, while import controls and a depreciation of the pound would add to the pressures on wages.

How can this problem be dealt with within an AES? The answer certainly does not lie in the adoption of a traditional incomes policy. When imposed against working-class opposition it has not only divided and weakened the Labour movement, but has proved ineffective in controlling inflation except in the short run. To develop an approach towards incomes it is helpful to examine the experience of the 'Social Contract' between the TUC and the Labour Party and subsequently the Labour Government.

The joint statement from the TUC–Labour Party Liaison Committee in February 1973, which set out the terms of the Social Contract for the first time, suggested that: "The problem of inflation can be properly considered only within the context of a coherent economic and social strategy." This context, however, proves on examination to be less coherent, and certainly less revolutionary, than was implied. The entire emphasis on the government side of the Contract was on administrative action on prices, rents and fares and redistribution through the tax system. It amounted to little more than a statement of a general intent to control Capital.

There was an explicit disavowal of any role for the state in promoting industrial democracy.

By the time of the October 1974 election manifesto, this vagueness had intensified. The Social Contract was presented as a democratic alternative to 'authoritarian incomes policies', and allegedly contained agreement on a 'whole range of national policies'. No details, however, were provided. Even the TUC itself in its parallel statement 'Collective Bargaining and the Social Contract' made only passing references to industrial investment, and none at all to trade policy; it explicitly accepted the logic of reducing inflation as *precondition* for renewed growth in national income.

Finally, even general references to a coherent economic strategy disappeared with the inauguration of the £6 policy in 1975. The Government document promulgating the policy – *'Attack on Inflation: a Policy for Survival'* – made no reference at all to any policies except those relating specifically to prices and incomes. It ended instead with a classic appeal by Wilson, in the long tradition of bourgeois politicians, to the Dunkirk spirit:

'The Government realises that the nation, realising the grim alternatives, will accept the sacrifices and play its part in the fight against inflation with courage and determination."

Of course, it is also the form, and not simply the content, of incomes policy in this period which we wish to criticise. The form of the Social Contract – a contract arranged between the Government and the national trade union leadership – set up contradictions which eventually destroyed both the contract and the Government. This emphasises the point that free collective bargaining is not simply a means of income determination – it is also rooted in a specific power arrangement inside the trade union movement. Institutional factors, especially the power of the shop stewards' organisation, are all-important here. The relative power of shop stewards was, we suggest, crucial in determining the direction of both TGWU and NUPE policy (in particular) after 1977.

From this discussion we can suggest certain principles which might guide the determination of incomes under an AES.

Firstly, it would take place in the context of progress on the AES as a whole. This would involve a substantial extension of public ownership, increased industrial investment, reflation of the economy and the introduction of import controls. But it would also involve specific measures to control prices and dividends, and to redistribute incomes both through the tax system and through direct action on high and low gross incomes. Second, it would take the form of an agreement in which all levels of the trade union movement part-icipated—above all, shop stewards and convenors. If an under-standing of this kind could not be reached as part of the AES, then frankly it might be better not to try to implement the strategy at all—better not to risk the major defeat for the working class which would be inevitable.

Third, there would be a presupposition that any agreement on incomes would seek to guarentee that the share of wages in total income was not reduced and that consequently growth in real gross wages would be ensured except in the circumstances of an uncontrolled fall in the terms of trade. *Finally*, any restriction in freedom to bargain over wages should be matched by an increase in control through trade union channels of the full range of strategic decisions within the enterprise—an extension of collective bargaining far beyond wages and conditions.

## 6. Conclusion: A Strategy For Controlling Inflation

The control of inflation will be a serious problem for a govern-ment implementing an AES. From an understanding of the source of inflation in conflicts over distribution between Capital and Labour, we have argued for control of inflation through a resolution of these conflicts in favour of Labour. We conclude by emphasising the need for a comprehensive and detailed strategy rather than ad hoc inter-vention. We have concentrated on the area of income determination because this is the most contentious but it is useful to draw together the strands of a comprehensive strategy.

1 There should be comprehensive and detailed price controls which take into account cost movements and investment requirements In large companies these could be negotiated through planning agreements.

2 There is a strong case for a temporary price freeze of six to twelve months to break the cycle of inflation.

3 There should be a broad agreement on income determination which conforms to the principles of extension of collective bar-gaining, guarantee of the wages share, involvement of shop stewards.

4 Prices should be brought down by some reduction in expenditure taxes, control of nationalised industry prices and subsidies on essentials.

5 Finally allocation of private credit should be brought under social control. This would not imply any reduction in the overall ex-pansion of credit.

# The AES: A political Strategy for Socialism

In previous chapters we argued that the AES is a technically coherent and feasible economic strategy for reversing Britain's economic decline and growing unemployment. But the AES is not only an economic strategy — it is also a political strategy with radical implications. In this chapter we take up the politics of economic strategy. We consider the political effects of introducing an alternative economic strategy, the importance of mobilising popular support for it, and the political opposition it is bound to encounter.

But in what sense is such a strategy socialist? Is it not just a variant of the social democratic project of managed welfare capitalism, or a recipe for an oppressive corporatism? We think that the key questions which must be asked are first whether the strategy seeks to challenge and progressively transform the constraints imposed by established economic and political structures, rather than pursue limited gains within these constraints. The second criterion is whether the strategy takes as fundamental the conflict between Capital and Labour and thus sees policy in political rather than in solely technical terms. Last we must ask if the strategy seeks to generate political mobilisation and raise political consciousness by making proposals which can be quickly realised and which meet present concerns, within a framework for medium and long term changes which move the economy toward socialism. We argue below that by asking these questions it is possible to distinguish our presentation of the AES clearly from a social democratic or simple reformist one.

## 1. Opposition And Offensive

The present Tory government is mounting a concerted attack on the working class through its economic and industrial policies, through cuts in public expenditure, through its industrial relations legislation, and through a redirection of the forces of 'law and order'. In each case the objective is to drive wedges between different sections of the working class—between the unemployed and those who are working, between skilled and unskilled workers, between the public and private sector and between trade unionists and others.

Thus it is vitally important that the defensive struggles that are fought against this attack—principally against cuts and against redundancies—are integrated within a framework that at the same time makes clear the underlying unity of interest between different struggles and the possibility of an *alternative* set of policies. To take just two examples, a successful fight against the closure of a particular hospital will only mean that cuts are transferred to other areas where the defence is less well organised—as long as the overall spending plans and cash limits remain in force. Thus fights against cuts must be brought together in support of a strategy that can guarantee an *increase* in spending. Similarly, in the fight against closures in the steel industry it is essential that the Labour movement develop an alternative approach which can ensure a future for threatened steel plants. This requires a plan for expansion of steel-using sectors, for regulation of trade in steel and for reinvestment in steel. The steel industry, perhaps more than most, cannot be considered in isolation from the rest of the economy, so a plan for steel would be of little use without an AES.

There are, however, many difficulties in linking defensive struggles into mobilisation around a broad alternative. It could be argued that there is little prospect of the Tories being removed from office, and so the best hope of moderating the damaging impact of their policies is to argue for modifications of policy which could conceivably be implemented by a Conservative Government—a bit more regional aid, job subsidies and possibly import controls. To gain support for these modifications they have to be presented as sensible changes in policy and not as a radical political alternative. This point of view is reflected in the current approach of the Labour and TUC leadership. The result, however, is that alternative policies for the Tories and the policies of a socialist alternative for Labour are often confused. It is crucial that we draw a clear distinction between them.

## 2. The AES As A Strategic Response To The Crisis

We feel strongly that what has been missing from much debate about economic policy on the 'parliamentary' Left in Britain has been an understanding of the profound break or 'rupture' that a socialist economic strategy represents. There is a tendency to personify the opposition to socialist policies and ascribe it to the Civil Service, 'the City', the IMF or the gnomes of Zurich.

Certainly the opposition expressed through these channels is important but we would argue that ultimately the constraints are more deeply embedded in the system. Capitalism – however much it is modified by the activities of the public sector – operates according to a certain logic or 'dynamic'. Within this capitalist dynamic there is very limited scope for action, and discussion of 'alternatives' is limited to debates about marginal variations in the values of particular variables – the value of the Public Sector Borrowing Requirement, the level of sterling etc. Unpopular policies become 'economically necessary', and these arguments are given strength because the real arguments about 'resources' (which any socialist government must face) are confused with arguments about the institutional structure within which those resources are disposed. Public spending 'must' be cut to reduce public borrowing and prevent interest rates rising, while alternative policies are sometimes referred to as challenging the 'laws of arithmetic'.

We can illustrate this point first by looking at the proposals for reflation which are central to the AES. The mid-seventies saw growing support for the view that fiscal policy could no longer be used to reduce the level of unemployment. Callaghan's famous statement to the Labour Party Conference in 1976 effectively marked the renunciation of the goal of full employment. But were the obstacles to reflation to achieve full employment technical or political? We would argue that the claimed technical obstacles – the difficulties of funding a larger budget deficit, the threat to the balance of payments, etc. were founded on the fundamental political judgement that the conflict between Capital and Labour, expressed in a rising level of inflation, could not be resolved at a high level of employment. Callaghan's statement amounted to a renunciation not simply of the goal of 'full employment' but also of any attempt to change the basis and the criteria which determine decisions about production.

## 3. The Constraints On Economic Reforms

The experience of recent Labour governments has made it clear that there are serious constraints upon the range and character of policies that a reforming government can introduce. If it accepts as a premise that investment in private industry must be left for management to decide, that the market must be the basic guide of what is produced, that there will be 'free' trade and freedom for capital to move overseas—then the room for introducing economic reforms in the interests of working people will be severely limited. If profit remains the mainspring of the private sector, determining investment, production and jobs, then sooner or later that Labour government will be compelled to take measures to raise profits, and to limit the aspirations and militancy of trade unionists. If it does not, then investment will fall in private industry, 'confidence' will be low and production in the capitalist sector will stagnate. Either way the working class will suffer the consequences. The logic cannot be broken by piecemeal interventions or ad hoc manoeuvres.

This is why we stress the importance of taking the AES as an interlocking whole which anticipates conflicts and offers a strategic response to the crisis. It seeks to change the dynamic of the economy, by inserting different criteria and interests in the way that many key decisions are taken. For example, it seeks to introduce controls on the movement of capital, and subject industrial investment to planning criteria. It involves workers and government planners in the decisions on investment and location of large companies, drawing upon the initiatives already taken by various groups of workers and shop stewards. It seeks to introduce social planning criteria into the determination of international trade, thus making international trade not master but servant of the needs of the economy.

The AES is constructed around measures to overcome the technical obstacles to reflation. A simple reflation of the economy *would* be subject to the constraints mentioned above. The AES thus incorporates measures to deal with trade, financing of government debt, and prices. Moreover, simple short term demand management *is* inadequate for dealing with structural problems of industry. The Tories are right in recognising the need to act on 'the supply side'. Their rhetoric however combines a naive faith in the efficiency of the market and personal incentive with a realistic assessment of the role of class struggle in production. But in constructing a comprehensive strategy for overcoming these 'technical' constraints, the AES mounts a fundamental challenge to the underlying political structure.

We must recognise that one 'Left' policy—such as an increase in public spending to finance local services, or an interventionist industrial strategy—will set in train a series of responses from Capital which will demand a coherent strategic response from the Left. This in turn will bring forward a new set of actions and responses. The AES will stand or fall as a *whole*; any attempt to rely on only one element—such as increases in public spending or import controls alone—will almost certainly fail. Thus we argue that the AES marks a political break with the logic of the capitalist dynamic of the economy and in this sense it is transitional.

## 4. Political Consciousness

If, as we argue, the AES represents a transitional socialist strategy, how does it relate to the development of political consciousness? Our view (in contrast to some other views held on the Left) is that political consciousness is best developed through collective organisation in struggle over realisable gains. It is a long-term process in which the forms of political organisation and the social relations they engender must anticipate or 'prefigure' the social relations intended as the outcome. It is a process which can build on transitional economic forms, those sectors and activities within capitalism which operate according to a different logic—which challenge the market determination of production or which establish new social relations. To take one example, the National Health Service—although in a distorted way—provides medical treatment according to need rather than according to the ability to pay.

Our reading of recent political history suggests that a broad radical socialist movement in Britain will not spring from crisis or from defeats, the outcome of which is far more likely to be apathy and disillusion. Nor will it be created by counterposing a 'programme'—constructed from first principles—to the 'misguided' policies to which the Labour movement retains a persistent attachment. Propaganda and persuasion play only a limited (albeit necessary and important) part in developing political consciousness. Equally important is people's lived experience: by achieving real improvements through struggle over realisable objectives, people will gain the realisation that things can be different. It is that confidence and belief that there are real alternatives, that is an absolute precondition for the development of socialist ideas. That belief comes not just through an act of the imagination: it comes also from concrete experience. That is why we see the AES as creating the conditions for the renewal and spread of socialist ideas.

## 5. The Role Of The State

Finally it is clear that the AES is built around various forms of state intervention. The state plays a crucial role in the regulation of the economy, and since the level of economic activity is a major determinant of class struggle, the state is clearly a major weapon in that struggle. But is it naive to think that the state can act to further working class interests? Will the civil service — or even the army — obstruct the AES? Will people be alienated from the strategy because they see it as a strengthening of bureaucracy? These are questions which any discussion of socialist strategy must confront.

The state has been the focus of attention for marxists in recent years. This work has been valuable in highlighting the structural constraints on the way the state can intervene; the lack of neutrality in the way it intervenes; and the way the institutions of the state can distort and suppress effective democratic political expression. The lesson for the AES is that a Left government cannot merely pick up the levers of state economic policy. Precisely because economic policy is a political weapon, any attempt to use it will meet with political opposition. There will be considerable resistance within the state machine itself, for example, to any policy which threatens to undermine the existing social order. Nonetheless, there is some limited scope for pushing state policy in a progressive direction and taking steps to democratise the institutions of government.

However, many on the Left take the view that a democratically elected socialist government would be brought down or reduced to impotence as capital exercised its political, economic or even military strength. The conclusion is sometimes drawn that it is a waste of time to work for the election of such a government — or more seriously, it is highly dangerous because it leaves the working class unprepared to defend itself against the repression which might follow, or cultivates illusions in the potential for gains within a bourgeois political system. The lesson of Chile is often quoted.

These are serious charges which cannot be dismissed. But it must be said that *any* strategy for socialist advance will meet with political opposition from those whose interests are threatened. The danger of political resistance to an AES is not an argument for rejecting that strategy, but for asking the further question — are the chances of overcoming that opposition any greater in the context of an AES than through any other strategy? We would argue they are, precisely because we believe the AES is capable of mobilising popular support and generating political consciousness, and because the legitimacy accorded to a democratically elected government is an important part of the battle against capitalist resistance.

Under an AES, the state has an important role in seeking to democratise the process of (especially economic) policy-making. The development of the strategy will have to be widely understood, if it is to succeed in retaining the support it will require through the counter-attack. Mobilisation will need to have some clear point of application if it is not to be frittered away in ineffective gestures. The development of more democratic forms of policy-making through planning agreements and local struggles is one channel for this. Another channel is the development of the political role of working-class organisations, both through the existing trade union structure, and through new forms of organisation. Both have developed considerably in recent years. The role of the state will be to co-ordinate these pressures and respond to them. We do not see development outside the state structure as an *alternative* to — or even incompatible with — the AES. Some would argue that by struggling for a strategy in which the state plays a leading role we are detracting from the scope for direct mobilisation and action. We would argue on the other hand that the AES is a necessary condition for mobilisation. It provides a framework within which workers' plans and other local struggles stand a far greater chance of success.

## 6. Conclusion

The AES is not an easy road to socialism. There are no easy roads to socialism, but, for the working class, there are no easy roads without it. The era of slowly but steadily rising living standards ended in the early seventies. With it died the image of a welfare state which ensured almost everyone a job and adequate public services. The organised power of the working class was enough to wound capital but not to break it finally. The resolution of what we have called the crisis will either restore Capital to health by weakening the working class, or it will see a decisive advance towards socialism. The AES is designed to provide the framework for the latter resolution.

The AES starts from concrete problems like jobs, living standards and public services. A direct attack on these problems is not a technical exercise: it will run into political and economic obstacles inherent in the nature of capitalist society. The combined forces of the press, the City and the Civil Service will at the same time attack the strategy, and try to divert and co-opt it. To succeed, therefore, the strategy has two requirements: support to overcome this opposition, and a clear understanding of the nature of the conflict. Just as the opposition would not be confined to parliamentary channels, so the mobilisation of support for an AES cannot be restricted to the confines of Westminster.

In this book we have not tried to lay down a programme or set out a simple formula. While defending the substance of the AES we have raised a range of issues which we believe need to be debated thoroughly in the Labour movement in the coming years. The choice is a simple one. We can either trim our policies to win the fragile 'confidence' of industrialists and financiers at home and abroad – a course which leads inevitably to the abandonment of social priorities and attempts to curb trade unions. Or we can make a clear break with the capitalist logic of the economy and initiate a process of socialist transformation.

The AES will certainly not introduce a socialist economy; but instead of being passive spectators and victims, people will have moved forward in the struggle of making their own history.

# APPENDIX: SOURCES AND FURTHER READING

In writing this book we have drawn heavily on publications from different sections of the Labour movement. In this Appendix we list some of our sources and some texts which offer more extended discussion or criticism of the issues we have taken up.

## Party publications

Statements of versions of the AES and discussions of different aspects of it can be found in publications from the Labour Party and Communist Party. Useful sources are:

Labour Party    *Labour and Industry* (1975)
                *Labour's Programme 1976*
                *International Big Business* (1977)
                *Peace Jobs Freedom* (1980)
                *Draft Manifesto* (1980)
*Labour Party Economic Review* (Bimonthly since September 1979)
Communist Party Economic Committee—*Economic Bulletin*

## Trade Unions

There are important statements published by the TUC and by individual trade unions. Recent publications include:

TUC:            *Economic Review* (published annually in February)
                *The Crisis of Monetarism and the TUC Alternative* (1980)
                *Employment and Technology* (1979)
                *The Role of Financial Institutions* (1979)
TUC-Labour      *Annual Statements*
Party Liaison   *Trade and Industry* (1980)
Committee
ASTMS           *Quarterly Economic Review*—various issues
AUEW-TASS       *Import Controls Now?* (1980)
CPSA/SCPS       *The Case Against the Cuts*
NUPE            *North Sea Oil and Economic Strategy* (1978)
TGWU            *Microelectronics* (1979)
                *Textiles and Clothing—The Fight For Survival* (1980)

## Discussions of Alternative Strategy

Four early presentations of the ideas in the AES can be found in:

Barratt Brown et al.—*An Alternative* Spokesmen Pamphlet 47, (Nottingham, 1975).

Cambridge Political Economy Group—*Britain's Economic Crisis* Spokesman Pamphlet 44, (Nottingham, 1974).

Holland S.—*The Socialist Challenge* (Quartet, London, 1975).

Sedgemore B.—*The How and Why of Socialism*, Spokesman Pamphlet, (Nottingham, 1977).

More recent discussions are included in:

Benn T.—*Arguments for Socialism* (Cape, London, 1979).

Blake D. and Ormerod P. (eds)—*The Economics of Prosperity* (Grant McIntyre, London, 1980).

Coates K. (ed)—*What Went Wrong* (Spokesman, Nottingham, 1979).

Hodgson G.—*Socialist Economic Strategy* (ILP, Square One Pub., Leeds, 1979).

Labour Coordinating Committee—*There is an Alternative* (LCC, 9 Poland St., London, 1980).

London CSE Group—'Crisis, the Labour Movement and the Alternative Economic Strategy' in *Capital and Class*, Summer 1979.

Prior M. and Purdy D.—*Out of the Ghetto* (Spokesman, Nottingham, 1979).

**Critical Discussions**

The AES has become a focus for a criticism from the Left. The following are some useful sources:

Bearman J.—'Anatomy of the Bennite Left' *International Socialism*, 2:6 Autumn 1979.

CSE State Group—Struggle over the State (CSE Books, London, 1979).

Freeman A.—'The Alternative Economic Strategy: a Critique' *International*, 1980.

Glynn A.—*Tribune's 'Alternative Strategy' or Socialist Plan* (Militant, London, 1979).

**Academic Work**

Most economists seem to be too preoccupied with endlessly elaborating sophisticated but purely abstract models to be concerned with understanding and tackling the immense economic problems we face. Valuable material however can be found in these works:

Blackaby F. (ed)—*Deindustrialisation* (Heinemann, London, 1979).

Cambridge Economic Policy Group—*Economic Policy Review* Cambridge Department of Applied Economics (Annual).

Major R. (ed)—*Britain's Trade and Exchange Rate Policy* (Heinemann, London, 1979).

National Institute for Economic and Social Research—*Economic Review*, (Quarterly).

*Cambridge Journal of Economics*. (Academic Press, London, Quarterly).

## Rank and file responses to the economic crisis

A number of alternative plans for specific companies or industries have recently been put forward by groups of shop stewards. The following is a brief list:

Leyland Combine T.U. Committee (1979)—*The Edwardes Plan and Your Job*

IWC Motors Group—*A Workers' Inquiry into the Motor Industry* (CSE Books, London, 1979).

Beynon H. and Wainwright H.—*The Workers' Report on Vickers*, (Pluto Press, London, 1979).

Lucas Aerospace Shop Stewards Combine Committee—*Lucas: An Alternative Plan*, Spokesman Pamphlet No. 55.

## CSE Books

CSE Books was founded by members of the Conference of Socialist Economists to promote the practical criticism of capitalism which the CSE as a whole is committed to and to facilitate wider participation in the debate and analysis going on in the CSE. Rather than forming ourselves into an academic editorial committee which sits in judgement of authors and in ignorance of readers, we want to engage politically in current debates and struggles. By coordinating with CSE activities in general, by publishing *Head & Hand: A Socialist Review of Books*, and by organising dayschools on issues thrown up by our own publications, we hope to narrow the gap which exists in bourgeois society between the producers and consumers of books.

For further information on CSE Books titles and the CSE Bookclub, write to 55 Mount Pleasant, London WC1X 0AE.

## New Titles

*Living Thinkwork: Where Do Labour Processes Come From?* Mike Hales.

Mike Hales describes his experience doing operations research at ICI, where even mental workers learn that ultimately 'You're not paid to think'. Through an account of 'scientific' work in a capitalist firm, his book shows the place of knowledge-production in the politics of management. A concrete intervention in Marxist theory of the labour process, this book is also a document in the history of the 'class of '68', exploring the contradictory social relations between theory and personal experience, theory and practice, and academic and industrial work. 192 pages illust.
Hb 0 906336 14 7 £10/Pb 0 906336 15 5 £3.50.

*Northern Ireland: Between Civil Rights and Civil War*, Liam O'Dowd, Bill Rolston & Mike Tomlinson.

This book is the first major study to document the origins and nature of Direct Rule in Northern Ireland, particularly the social-democratic model which Britain has attempted to superimpose upon the Orange State. The authors argue that Direct Rule has not been overcoming the notorious sectarianism of Stormont but has instead reconstituted class sectarian relations more subtlely within the new state institutions. Their argument is illustrated through detailed studies of the economy, trade unions, local government, housing, community politics and repression.
Hb 0 906336 18 X £12/Pb 0 906336 19 8 £3.95.